Pacific Ocean

PRACTICE AREA

Surveyed and Depicted by
John Grant
Golf Course Architect

THE
GOOD
DOCTOR
RETURNS

a novel by

Geoff Shackelford

Sleeping Bear Press
Chelsea, Michigan

Sleeping Bear Press
121 South Main Street
P.O. Box 20
Chelsea, MI 48118

Printed and bound in the United States

10 9 8 7 6 5 4 3 2 1

Cataloguing-in-Publication Data

Shackelford, Geoff D.
The good doctor returns / Geoff D. Shackelford.
p. cm.
ISBN 1-886947-43-0
1. Mackenzie, A. (Alexander), b. 1870--Fiction. 2. Golf courses--Design
and construction--Fiction. I. Title.
PS3569.H27G6 1998
813'.54--dc21   98-13302
CIP

Also by Geoff Shackelford

The Riviera Country Club...A Definitive History

The Captain

Masters of the Links

For Ruggles — *A great friend*

1

$\mathcal{I}$ could feel the gray-walled cubicle closing in after another long day in the high-rise offices of Mario International Golf Course Design. At the moment, my attention was focused on a set of blueprints my boss had returned earlier in the day to my already–overloaded desktop.

As usual, the architectural alterations made by my world-renowned boss, William "Bill" Mario, had forced me to ponder my future. Like any normal 27-year-old, I wondered about, among other things, the meaning of my life and what I was going to do about my miserable job that most people would kill for.

For as long as I can remember, I've had an enduring fascination with the art of golf course design, always dreaming of maybe one day becoming a successful architect. I've read, reread, highlighted, and dog-eared the classic golf architecture books by master architects like Alister MacKenzie, George Thomas, Robert Hunter and Charles Blair Macdonald. More recently, I have purchased and studied books by Bill Mario's competitors, like Robert Trent Jones Jr., Michael Hurdzan and Tom Doak. I study them intently despite warnings from Bill, who seems to think I am so naïve that reading about what our competitors were doing might sabotage my young mind.

When any of the major golf publications arrive in the mail I read them from cover to cover immediately. After making notations for my personal files on new projects or other news from the architecture world, I clip and file away the articles in blue-topped computer-label files. My collection covers every architect known to man, from the very first professional designer, Old Tom Morris, to a modern day eccentric like Pete Dye. I've clipped thousands of photographs of good and bad examples of golf design for personal reference — waiting for that day when I'll have my own design firm and I might need a piece of information dealing with a specific situation I might encounter.

I grew up in a middle-class Northern California home and attended the University of Arizona on a partial golf scholarship. I originally majored in landscape architecture with golf course design in the back of my mind, but as a bright-eyed freshman I was determined to become a Tour player. Who wouldn't want to play the Tour and travel to heavenly places every week and hang out with the beautiful people?

However, as a part-time starter my first two years, I saw the Tour dream begin to slip away as I watched my more talented teammates (and future Tour players) Robert Gamez and David Berganio make the game look way too effortless. I also had a problem with my wild imagination. It began to interfere with my ability to keep the game simple, leading me down some pretty oddball roads in a futile attempt to perfect my swing. In the process, I lost sight of what competitive golf was really all about: scoring.

After missing more team tournaments than I had qualified for, I slowly turned to my old passion: golf course design. I was spurred on by the lack of architectural merit of the desert layouts U of A played in golf course–heavy Tucson. I pledged to return someday and build something respectable for my alma mater so they could compete for the top recruits with Arizona State, which tends to land better players. My theory was that Scottsdale had a more enticing array of golf courses, giving ASU an edge.

When the time arrived after graduation to interview for work, I knew that my solid golf game and my ability to communicate well would help my chances. In the competitive environment of modern day golf architecture, architects figure they need every advantage they can get to sway potential clients, so they like having a scratch golfer on staff to somehow convince customers that playing ability is vital to designing a decent course. It's ridiculous that one's handicap would have anything to do with hiring somebody to perform a highly artistic and technical job, but when you are trying to break into an extremely competitive business you take what you've been blessed with and use it to your advantage.

After interviews with five firms, I decided the best opportunity appeared to be an entry-level design associate position with Mario International Golf Course Design, though it appealed to me for all the wrong reasons.

I thought I could benefit from William Brent Mario's name. (That was the name he went by until recently because he thought it sounded similar to Robert Trent Jones. Now that Tom Fazio is the hottest architect in the business, Bill has condensed his name, evidently hoping someone might confuse the two).

You see, Bill was a recent recipient of *Global Golf's* "Architect of the Year." The magazine always gives its award to the most "newsworthy" architect each year, regardless of the true merits of the candidate's work. In Bill's case, a nasty split with his one-time Tour player–architect associate, Billy Hatch, put him in the headlines and earned him Architect of the Year. Amazingly, most of Bill's clients didn't read the article on the award, so they don't understand that he won under such inauspicious circumstances.

Nonetheless, part of my rationale in taking the position wasn't half bad. I assumed that a job with a "name" architect would look great on my résumé and might propel me into the upper reaches of the business sooner than a higher-level position with a lesser-known architect.

During my first few months at Mario International Design's Los Angeles headquarters, I studied and preserved all of Bill's discarded sketches and leftover blueprints. After all, my boss was considered a genius by those who were supposed to know, wasn't he?

But after a few days like today, it dawned on me that my boss cared little about the game of golf and even less about interesting golf course design. Once a hardworking and creative architect, the great Bill Mario had become a mere salesman, as indicated by his latest changes to my preliminary drawings for a new development in Central California's San Luis Obispo, with the hideous working title of Pigeon Run Golf Course.

I'm paid $45,000 a year to put up with his stupidity, but what Bill did today was just plain sad. He had taken one of my carefully sketched dogleg left par-4's and stripped it of any semblance of architectural integrity. In my version, a troublesome bunker was placed about 240 yards from the tee at the corner of a dogleg left, with another trap placed to guard the front right of the putting surface. This meant that the golfer who dared and succeeded in carrying the fairway bunker would be rewarded with an open shot to the green, virtually eliminating a more difficult shot over the greenside hazard.

Meanwhile, the player who drove away from my fairway bunker would be forced to hit a longer and more difficult shot to the putting surface.

We are not talking about brain surgery here. It was the most basic of strategic par-4's — straight from the Donald Ross or MacKenzie schools of design.

Mario disagreed. And he chose the worst possible time to rearrange preliminary plans: five days before proposals were due. In his infinite wisdom Bill decided that the fairway should be pinched with two traps on each side of the landing area 260 yards from the tee, in order to, as he put it, "celebrate the style of Robert Trent Jones." I guess someone forgot to tell Bill that frankly, it wasn't too wise to copy old Trent's style anymore.

It gets worse. Next, Bill crossed out my version of the green complex and told me to replace it with the computer model of number fifteen at the TPC at Forest Quarry, a critically acclaimed earlier design of Mario's. Bill suggested that I take the green "as-builts" from Forest Quarry off the computer to save some time.

"That green at Forest Quarry really drains well," Bill said, as justification for grabbing the green off the computer instead of creating something slightly original.

For me, as someone who reveres and respects the game of golf, this was an outrage. To make matters worse, the terrain for the proposed green site at Pigeon Run (elevated) was completely different from the TPC (flat ground).

In the past, I suspected that Bill was burned out and void of any more creativity; this latest alteration proved it. It was clear that Mario no longer cared about strategic design or encouraging a golfer to use his brain. Bill wanted to save time and money and make his courses as difficult as possible because the magazine ranking panelists tend to remember the tougher, well-conditioned layouts. Sadly, most of the developers who employ Mario like it that way — difficult courses that look almost identical to the last award winner he built.

In recent months, Mario showed less and less shame about his lack of creativity and more interest in justifying his design fee increase from $500,000 to $700,000. He was merely trying to survive — oh, and make as much money as possible.

When Bill Mario started his golf architecture career as a construction supervisor for famed architect Dick Wilson, some attention was still devoted to creating unique golf holes. Fieldwork was still part of the business back then. Holes were frequently tinkered with after construction commenced if the architect had an idea to make the hole better, or, perhaps, because the land didn't quite fit with what had been put down on paper. However, as it became more lucrative over the years to whip out the courses in assembly-line fashion, Bill lost interest in the artistic side and focused on building his business empire.

Personally, I have no argument with Bill's desire to make money. But days like this one, when out of sheer laziness, he crushed any hint of originality, told me that I would not find my hoped-for on-the-job education in the offices of Bill Mario. That did not bother me as much as the suspicion that I would not find it in any other office. Perhaps my standards were too high. Maybe I should just take the money and find pleasure from other things in life, like my nice car or my apartment near the beach.

$\mathcal{I}$ staggered home at eight o'clock, in a state of deep depression, after making the changes Bill ordered. Instead of tossing a light salad and reading up on the new pesticides from a book I had just ordered, I opted for my version of Prozac. I phoned Dominoes to order a medium mushroom pizza and then slipped my favorite movie into the VCR, *Midnight Run*. I shoved aside the pile of bills on my couch and settled in for an evening of pure, unadulterated mental vegetation.

While Robert DeNiro and Charles Grodin bickered their way cross-country, my mind kept gravitating toward thoughts about the job and how far it had strayed from my imaginary ideal. Bill Mario had one of the most envied positions in golf: the ability to pick and choose almost any project he wanted and the budgets to design wildly innovative holes that golfers would yearn to play. Yet the man simply came to the office, talked incessantly on the phone with marketing people and reporters, marked up a few plans with stupid changes, perused the *Robb Report*, then went home having done absolutely nothing creative at all.

Perhaps the years of hassling with environmentalists, planning commissions, construction companies and irate country club members had stripped Mario of the energy to stay fresh. He lived to satisfy his bank account, not the golfers he was well compensated to challenge with thoughtful designs. And I could see how government regulations and environmental lobbies might have taken the fun out of the business. But there still had to be a way to build excellent golf courses without compromising the game and the golfers who pay way too much money these days to play a round of golf.

Sometimes I wonder if my frustration is merely a symptom of my being only twenty-seven. Or maybe modern golf course design has become an irrational business with the creative and inventive sides permanently lost to a bunch of engineers. After all, the golfers aren't complaining. Courses are in better condition than ever and golf is booming. Of course, special effects in the movies are more amazing than ever, and motion pictures are grossing more money than ever, but that doesn't mean they are satisfying to watch. We have a lot of *Independence Day* golf courses, and not too many you can label *The Godfather* of golf course design.

I guess what I've struggled with most is how my heroes, like Alister MacKenzie and Donald Ross, who produced so many great courses, spent little or no time on-site and still stuck to their principles. Could they do it today, or would developers continue to want something larger and more obnoxious than what was built down the street?

Upon circling back to this persistent question, I knew that another review of my own or Bill Mario's life was pointless. I was making good money, had my health, and no real reason to complain. There were starving people in China for Christ's sake!

Not even feeling guilty that I had devoured the entire medium pizza, I continued vegetating by picking up the funniest book of all time, Dan Jenkins' *You Gotta Play Hurt*. The reading didn't prove to be easy, with my eyes burning from another day under those damned flickering fluorescent office lights. I struggled to keep my eyelids open, but my head began dizzily lolling against the back of my couch. As I settled into one of my favorite pastimes — sleeping — I heard the sound of my phone ringing, and I think I remember answering.

"John Grant?" the oddly Americanized Scottish accent asked.

I hate it when people I don't know call and know my name.

"Yes?" I said abruptly.

"I understand you have a thorough knowledge of all that has happened to golf course construction: environmental legislation, USGA green specifications, cart paths, automatic irrigation systems, and God knows what else you people have to deal with in the 90s," the voice said with a note of challenge.

"Yes I do, actually," I replied. As soon as I said it, something warned me that I was making a fool of myself by answering this call.

"Well, I'm looking for someone to help me get back into the design business, and I need someone like you," the man replied.

"Who is this?" I demanded, upset that I had been disturbed by an apparent prank call.

"If you listen to what I have to say, you might just learn a thing or two."

Now I was cranky. "I'm too tired for this — I'm hanging up."

"My name is Dr. Alister MacKenzie, and I'm restarting my business."

I had to roll my eyes at that one. I hit "pause" on the VCR remote control.

"Yeah?" I replied, "Well I'm Scott Hoch and I just love the Old Course at St. Andrews."

Deep silence from the other end. I love well-timed sarcasm.

"That boy Hoch called it a cow pasture, didn't he?" the man asked.

"Look, I've got things to do. Who's the comedian?" I asked, trying to remember which associate in the firm even knew that Alister MacKenzie was Scottish, much less a golf architect.

"I expected that kind of response," the man replied calmly. This was getting old. "I'm hanging up now."

"Well, if you want to practice genuine golf architecture," the voice said, "meet me Saturday morning in the superintendent's office at The Valley Club of Montecito. They say it's only a ninety-minute automobile drive from where you are. Amazing things these autos have become."

Someone was really hard up for entertainment. This was the best they could come up with? Faking a dead guy's voice at 10:30 p.m. on a Thursday night? "Well, thanks but no thanks," I retorted.

"Your loss, young man," the voice returned. "Please give it some consideration. It might be the cure for some of your misery."

Why hadn't I hung up yet? "Goodbye. I've had a long day," I said wearily, finally placing the phone down on the hook. I assumed it was one of the guys in the office with way too much free time on his hands. But as I "unpaused" *Midnight Run*, I had a strange feeling about the crank call. The man's voice sounded ancient, and even more strangely, it sounded sincere.

2

$\mathcal{J}$ spent Friday at the office obediently preparing new plans to submit to Bill. The revised set would include narrowed–down landing areas and putting greens regurgitated from the computer. The Pigeon Run bid had to be submitted by Monday morning at a law office in San Luis Obispo, so I didn't have time to try to change Bill's mind.

All day I pondered the prank call from the night before. Which jokester was it? Who in the firm actually knew Alister MacKenzie's name, much less that he had designed The Valley Club? And who could imitate that gritty, alcohol-worn Scottish accent?

"I don't have time for this crap," I swore to myself, hastily shoving aside the mound of paperwork on my desk, trying to forget about Alister MacKenzie.

That afternoon I made final preparations to submit the cloned plans, which, of course, Bill had overwhelmingly approved before leaving at 1:30 to go cigar shopping. I made duplicates and packed up copies of the pro-forma and other blueprints for my trip to San Luis Obispo. I was supposed to drive north on Sunday afternoon and spend the night at a motel before submitting the highly coveted Mario International Golf Course Design bid by Monday's noon deadline.

As I left the office, thoughts of the strange phone call persisted. No one at work even hinted that they had played a joke on me, and I was not about to make an ass of myself by asking who had called me at home impersonating Doctor Alister MacKenzie.

But the more I thought about it, the more I considered leaving for San Luis Obispo a day early. After all, lovely Montecito was halfway to San Luis and I could always stop for a sandwich at Pierre Lafond's Gourmet Market and hang out with the beautiful people, then drop by the Valley Club and pretend I was stopping in for a casual inspection of one of my favorite MacKenzie designs.

"I've lost my mind," I mumbled, shaking my head as I gathered my briefcase and all of the Pigeon Run paperwork.

There was a way I could do this without making a fool of myself. I would say hello to the Valley Club superintendent, whom I had met a few years ago at the Golf Course Superintendents Association of America convention. Because if there was any real connection to the Valley Club and the phone call, I would figure it out in Montecito. Besides, after the Valley Club, I could go over to one of the new Santa Barbara area courses for an inspection.

The solitude of the early Saturday morning drive up the California coast allowed me to reflect a bit more on my career. Practicing golf architecture was what I really wanted to do, yet the industry seemed to be in decline. In the passenger's seat lay another lousy Bill Mario design that everyone in the golf community would applaud. "Bill's done it again," they'd all say.

"What garbage...if they only knew," I said to myself, beginning to wonder if this tendency of talking out loud to myself was becoming a habit.

As my forest green Explorer neared the Highway 101, Sheffield Road off-ramp, I rehearsed my story for the Valley Club superintendent. There was a good possibility I was about to make a fool of myself, but nobody could accuse me of not being prepared.

As my sport utility vehicle handled the winding Sheffield Road, I was reminded that Montecito is one of the world's most beautiful communities, and that by comparison Los Angeles was becoming an uninhabitable nightmare.

Stately two-hundred-year-old oaks and sycamores shelter the rustic town of Montecito, or "the Village," as the more pretentious locals call it. Home to a mix of retired corporate chieftains, prominent Santa Barbara businessmen, and even a few Hollywood types, Montecito has only two traffic signals and one gas station. Many of the area estates hide behind tall hedges and line the meandering creek beds that help drain the towering mountains of the nearby Los Padres National Forest during the winter.

Alister MacKenzie and his one-time design associate, Robert Hunter, designed The Valley Club of Montecito in 1927 and opened it for play a year later. The 18-hole course features a set of eight holes in front of a brooding old English clubhouse. The white-with-gray-trim building sits atop a small rise overlooking the course; the Pacific Ocean can be seen less than a mile away. The club's comfortable stone patio sits above the first and sixteenth tees and has views of the first, fifteenth and eighteenth greens. The remaining ten holes occupy stunning terrain across the tiny two-lane Sheffield Road, with the ninth green sitting at the northeastern end of the property.

The course contains an eclectic group of MacKenzie holes, with the eastern side of the layout hugging the base of an oak-and-brush-covered hill. The 6,500 yard design is dotted with hundreds of magnificent and yet unobtrusive trees. Best of all, it contains the usual MacKenzie design aura: playable and interesting for the average man, but challenging enough for the low-handicapper. That's a catch phrase used by all of the architects today, but MacKenzie was one of the few architects who could actually carry out that philosophy.

The greens at the Valley Club are extremely small and thus weren't built with the Doctor's typical severe undulations, though they do contain enough slope to add strategic interest to the course. MacKenzie and Hunter knew this would be a member's course, so they made sure to make it a joy to play on a regular basis.

The bunkers at The Valley Club scream MacKenzie. Though many have lost their original jagged and eye-catching impact after years of edging and other maintenance practices, their well-camouflaged construction and strategic placement remain almost identical to the opening day design.

Not a single hole at The Valley Club seems forced, and the routing of the holes provides several amusing surprises. The simple, rustic beauty of the course constantly astounds, with mountain views and a charming little creek coming into play on five holes. The early morning fog in Montecito and consistently clear blue afternoon skies are enhanced by the comfortable temperatures, which never seem to rise above 80 degrees or dip below 55.

The golf course maintenance building for The Valley Club sits on a tree-lined asphalt road just behind the par-3 fourth green. The building is hidden from view by flowering oleander bushes and overhanging sycamores. As I turned into the dirt courtyard in front of the building, I spotted a lone pickup truck. Through the building's windows I saw a man who appeared to be the superintendent, sitting at his desk doing some paperwork. It was only a few minutes after ten o'clock and it looked as if the maintenance staff had gone home, probably after mowing the greens and raking the bunkers early that morning.

As I got out of my Explorer and approached the small office, I again rehearsed my speech. Sitting behind the desk was Alex McDonald. Alex had approached me at Mario Design's convention booth because one of his members wanted some information on Bill in case they decided to bring in a professional architect to restore the course. McDonald and I, however, agreed that Bill Mario was not the man to meddle with an original MacKenzie design, and fortunately the job went to an architect with much more respect for "the Good Doctor."

As I approached the office an uneasy feeling of nervousness, sort of like first tee jitters, overtook me.

"Hi, Alex," I extended my hand. "John Grant." I received a typical firm handshake from the golf course superintendent. "Remember me? We met at last year's GCSAA convention."

"Of course, John. I've been expecting you."

"You have?"

"You're here to interview with Dr. MacKenzie, right?"

I nearly wet my pants. I tried a feeble rebuttal.

"Oh, so Alex, you're the jokester!" I said, feeling more awkward by the minute, my stomach tightening into a golfball-sized knot.

"Uh...what?" McDonald asked, looking bewildered. Considered pretty young to have such a prestigious superintendent's job, Alex was a very focused, straightforward man.

I finally stammered, "So really, why did you ask me here?"

"I didn't," McDonald protested. "Doctor MacKenzie did. He's working out of my office until he can get his business up and running again."

This wasn't funny anymore. "All right, the world doesn't need another comedian Alex, we've already got 50,000 of them out of work in L.A.," I chided.

McDonald shook his head. "If you don't believe me, go out to the fourth green and see him with your own eyes. He's the older gentleman driving around in the green golf cart."

I stared at him, too stunned to know what else to do.

"Go on," said McDonald, with a reassuring grin. "The old man doesn't bite."

3

"You must be John," the well-dressed old man said from underneath his traditional Scottish wool cap as I approached his golf cart. The Americanized-Scottish accent sounded even more authentic in person. Whoever he was, the old man was doing an amazing job of imitating Alister MacKenzie.

The beige plus-fours, the matching vest over a white shirt, the gold watch chain stretching from the left vest pocket to the right vest pocket, and the bold burgundy tie — very MacKenziesque. I also recognized the squarely trimmed mustache, the enormously overgrown eyebrows, and the man's funny gap-toothed grin as the MacKenzie I had seen in photographs. However, more interesting to me was the man's age. He had to be well over one hundred judging by his weathered skin, which clearly had spent way too many years under the sun.

"Glad you could come over today," the old man said rather seriously. He took off his hat, offered his wrinkled hand and slowly rose from his golf cart seat. "It's okay. I don't bite."

"Who are you?" I asked skeptically as I stepped up to the cart to shake his large hand.

"I told you," the old man said. "I'm Doctor Alister MacKenzie. I've decided to reestablish my design business here on the West Coast. Now, will you get over the shock of my presence so we can get down to business?"

I had to call this guy's bluff right away. "Do you *really* expect me to believe you are Alister MacKenzie? I happen to know he's been dead for over sixty years."

"Not so," the old man shook his head. "Just took a long vacation. You'll just have to take my word that I am who I say I am."

"So if you are Alister MacKenzie, then, uh...tell me about the manuscript you wrote but never published," I asked, making a second attempt to trip up this obvious imposter.

"Couldn't you come up with a tougher one than that?" the old man asked. "But I suppose we can play these games for a while, though it doesn't bode well for your future with MacKenzie and Associates — or I suppose it could even be MacKenzie and Grant, Inc."

"What are you talking about?" I scoffed.

The old man sat back down in his golf cart. "This was supposed to be an interview of you today, but if you must have some details about my life, then so be it," he grunted.

I tried a more respectful approach this time. "Sir, you have to understand that it's hard for me to accept that you are Alister MacKenzie."

"Well, don't say I didn't warn you," he said. "At the risk of boring you, here goes. *The Spirit of St. Andrews* would be the book I completed before I disappeared in 1934. I needed some money, since I had over $15,000 owed to me by clients, including some famous ones. Scribners in New York was my first choice to publish it because they had done a fine job with Bob Hunter's book, *The Links*. I sent the manuscript there, and was considering adding some more text on camouflage. I'm sure you know that was one of my areas of expertise and an important aspect of my work."

I nodded and went along with the imposter for a moment. "So, why didn't the manuscript get published?"

"As I said, Scribner's was indecisive — bloody New York publishers," the old man grumbled. "The Depression was at its peak, and before Scribner's made up their mind, I had decided to, well, disappear. So the manuscript sat in my stepson's desk for a number of years until I had my stepgrandson, Raymund, start a search for the bloody thing. Well, one night while I was at his home, I asked him to look through his father's old desk and what do you know? He found the bloody manuscript!"

The joyful look left the old man's face for a moment. "Of course the Scribner's copy was sitting neglected in the vault of a famous architect who I'd entrusted to care for Hilda when I disappeared — but that's another tedious story of an envious and jealous man and not deserving of our time."

I interrupted. "Why didn't you include the information on camouflage?"

"I decided it was worthy of a book in itself, which I'd write after *The Spirit of St. Andrews*. Unfortunately, my health and finances were declining so I never actually compiled the book, though most of it has been written and is just waiting to be put together."

"I had never heard that you wanted to put together another book."

"Well, now you have. Can we talk about you, John?"

"I'm still not satisfied you are who you say you are," I protested.

"You're as skeptical as I was at your age," the old man grinned. "I like that!"

I corrected him. "I'm not skeptical about everything, just about who you say you are."

"I understand," the old Scot said, trying to be patient. "So do you want the long, dull version of my life story? Or just an account of the lucrative California years?" he asked, his voice tinged with irony.

I presumed he was referring to MacKenzie's final years when he supposedly died broke.

"I want the whole thing," I said. "I have read every article ever written on MacKenzie and by MacKenzie, and believe me, I will know when you slip up, whoever you are."

The old man shrugged his shoulders and launched into his life story.

"I was born in Yorkshire, England, in 1870," the man recited as he gingerly rose from his cart and walked to the rear of the fourth green, taking a seat under the shade of a sprawling oak. "I spent my summers as a young man in the Highlands of Scotland in a small town called Lochinver. Lovely place, but no golf courses! I carried out my studies at Cambridge, where they gave me a Bachelor of Medicine and Surgery in 1895."

I tried to trip him up. "You really never were a practicing physician, were you?"

"That is somewhat correct, though I did serve as a field surgeon in the Boer War. What a horrific and messy affair, though war is war. It was especially sad because the British were so inept and unequipped to use nature for protection. I was astounded at the Boers' brilliant manipulation of the landscape. That led me to develop many of the camouflage theories I had originally thought up when we hunted the red deer in Lochinver. But much of what I learned came from the soldiers themselves. I'm proud to say these techniques later saved the lives of thousands of soldiers who hid themselves in the treeless fields during the First World War. At the time, it occurred to me that this might help me to visualize golf course design, and of course it later provided me with many ideas for strategic course design."

After the man's faultless start, I was impressed. Could this really be MacKenzie? How on earth could anyone live that long? Well, no sense in interrupting him. Perhaps he would slip up in a minute.

"Following the war, I worked in Leeds and separated from my first wife," the old imposter claimed. "In my spare time I played with models of greens and bunkers while serving on the committee preparing the Headingley Golf Club's new Alwoodley course. Of course, my ideas were brilliant, but the committee wouldn't take the advice of a local, so they brought in Harry Colt, who merely reinforced what I'd been saying all along!"

Cocky old bastard! This sounded like the MacKenzie I had read stories about. This guy was a good actor.

"Sometime around 1907, Colt stayed at my residence," he continued. "Of course, only recently have the members at Alwoodley started crediting me with the design, since I'm now a recognized 'name architect.' There were some nasty politics mixed in there, as my former wife was a prominent member of the club. But that is another story."

I could not believe what I was hearing. The more I stared into those squinty, weathered eyes, the more I began to wonder if this really might be MacKenzie. Still unsure, I tried to keep a non-committal look on my face, though the man's ease in sharing his life story made it clear he wasn't afraid of getting caught in a discrepancy.

"When Harry Colt stayed with me, we got on well, and he was open to my suggestions on Alwoodley," the old man continued. "We eventually worked on a few projects together, though as you know we went our own separate ways after the Great War."

"Yes, I read about that," I said, and then realized as the words slipped out that I had just cracked the facade of disbelief I was trying to maintain.

"How much do you know about our split?" the old man asked, slowly taking off his wool cap and rubbing his starkly bald head. He either hadn't noticed my slip or merely accepted the fact that I was convinced.

"Just what I've read," I replied, hoping to hear more. "Let's have your side."

"Well, I think some sort of jealousy began in 1914 when I submitted a drawing of a two-shotter for a *Country Life Magazine* contest, and I took first prize. I suppose Harry Colt was envious I won...I really don't know. I have my moments when I can be a bit stubborn — that certainly might have contributed as well."

Since I had already slipped, I interjected some information to let him know that I was well-read. "That contest was judged by Charles Blair Macdonald, architect of The National, wasn't it?" I asked, remembering reading about it in an old magazine article.

"Yes, and also by Horace Hutchinson, Herbert Fowler and Bernard Darwin. The hole was later constructed during the war by C.B. and Seth Raynor at the Lido course on Long Island."

"Was it a good hole?"

"John...if it pleased Macdonald, Hutchinson, Fowler and Darwin, I'd say it was a good hole. It beat eighty other entries, including those by Vardon and Ray — you know them? They are part of that crowd who fancies that if they can play well then they're automatically qualified to design a course."

"So, the prize-winning hole really was built?" I asked.

"Oh yes. When I was constructing the Bayside Links on Long Island, which has sadly disappeared, I saw the Lido and was impressed. Though they did modify my drawing for the final version to fit the terrain. Now, let me finish," the old man said, sensing that we were straying from the topic and that he was about to win me over.

"After I won the contest, I dissolved my medical practice and dabbled in golf course architecture, but war broke out again. The same day it was announced I had won the *Country Life* contest, I had to change my plans."

"Did you go to fight?" I asked.

"Heavens no!" he said. "But the British Army did call on my services, this time assigning me to the Royal Engineers, where I was allowed to expand on my camouflage techniques, which were eventually credited for saving thousands of British lives."

"What happened to you after the war?"

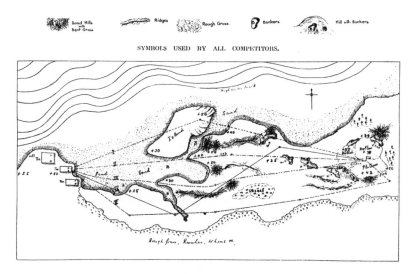

THE FIRST PRIZE DESIGN OF A TWO-SHOT HOLE, BY DR. A. MACKENZIE
Which won a golfing architecture competition in England for
three prizes given by Mr. C.B. Macdonald

"I finished some projects in the Isles before beginning to travel abroad. I worked independently and traveled extensively through England and spent several months in New Zealand and Australia during the 1920s. I was consulted on new designs, but mostly I was asked to improve many inferior club courses, though I rarely oversaw their construction."

"Why not?" I asked.

"Well, I found some talented local people like Alex Russell to oversee the work in Australia, and I didn't want to leave my home for a whole year. Besides, look how nice Royal Melbourne and the others turned out."

I tried to keep up the tough questions, but I didn't even know the answer to the next one. "When did you come to California?"

"Permanently? In the late 1920s. The available work in England was not very enticing, and my Scottish charm apparently wasn't taking too well with many of the committees I worked with," MacKenzie said, shaking his head.

I couldn't fight my smile on that one. MacKenzie was notorious for his blunt and often tactless manner with committees and clients. Some accounts hinted that he could be downright mean, but if this was in fact him, he had mellowed somewhat. After 128 years, I would hope so!

The old man continued. "I formed a partnership with Robert Hunter and the fine amateur champion Chandler Egan. Later Perry Maxwell worked for me on courses in the Midwest. The Valley Club and Cypress Point were done primarily with Bob Hunter, while the other Northern California courses were in collaboration with Bob, Chandler Egan and Jack Fleming.

"Later I traveled to the eastern United States and designed Augusta National with Bobby Jones; Bayside on Long Island by myself; and two courses in Michigan with Perry Maxwell's help. I also laid out a course for Ohio State University, which was built after my suppositious death at Pasatiempo in 1934. It was reported in the newspapers that my ashes were dropped from a plane over the course."

"So you never died?" I asked, still not quite believing what I was hearing.

"Of course not," he said.

"Then how old you are today?"

"That's a rude question, laddie, but if you must know, I'm 128."

Sure he was. How could anyone buy into such a ridiculous story? "So, how have you lived that long?" I asked, trying not to laugh.

"Aww, that's an ancient Scottish secret," he laughed. "But I certainly have cheated father time!"

This was getting weird, and aggravating. Part of me believed him, part of me could not believe I could be so gullible. As I looked him over, there was something about the scent of musty tobacco and alcohol on his clothes that made him seem so real.

"So, what have you been doing all this time?" I asked.

"First, I got my health in order," the old man answered quietly. "It was embarrassing to not be able to pay my bills and support my family. So I practiced medicine during the Second World War in Southern California, and eventually saved enough to do some traveling with my Hilda, who was most patient with me."

"Why did you go into hiding? And how come you left the design business?"

"I was very tired. The Depression was a terrible thing — I lost most of my money in the market — and it changed the way business was conducted. Golf architecture went from being a pleasurable art form to a competitive business, and I never really wanted to deal with the issues of modern golf and contemporary business. Health and happiness are everything in this world. Money-grubbing, or so-called business, except insofar as it helps attain health and happiness, is of minor importance to me."

"Have you seen your living relatives?" I asked.

"I've been staying in my grandson Raymund's house for some time," he said. "I've been doing a lot of reading, and during the summers I travel a bit when I feel well enough. When I started to read the modern publications, I was dismayed to see how society has declined, and I was appalled at what had become the standard in golf architecture. I told Ray that *The Spirit of St. Andrews* had to get published. When it was and we saw such a fine response, I started to get the itch to build a course again, and here I am."

"Sixty-some years is a long time to go into hiding," I observed doubtfully.

"It was, but I enjoyed it, and I was able to spend the remaining days with my lovely Hilda before she passed away. However, I think my own days are numbered now, and I want my final ones to be productive."

At 128, how many days does he think he has left?

"I figure it is worth the risk, and I can go out setting a fine example!" he continued. "Hell, these golf architects today couldn't polish my shoes, much less design a playable hole!"

I had no response to that final comment, wondering if my involvement with Mario International Golf Design placed me in that group too. Based on his reputation, it certainly was something you would expect to hear from the real Alister MacKenzie.

I was getting dizzy. He had all of the characteristics of the famed old Scot — probably the greatest golf architect of all time. He had the cockiness. The intelligence. The gruff style. The education. Was this really Doctor Alister MacKenzie in flesh and blood?

4

"So John, what kind of architect do you want to be?" the old man asked as we drove up the fifth fairway in his green cart. The fifth was a slightly uphill par-4 of 400 yards. There were three major bunkers to negotiate off the tee along with some overhanging oaks. The hazards were pretty easy to carry, and the hole had an eye-catching cross bunker about eighty yards from the green.

I began to notice more about the old man. There was an old leather-covered sketchbook tucked in the cart dashboard, and he had been working the cigarettes pretty hard because the ashtray was overflowing. Sitting right next to him, I noticed the smell of whiskey and cigarettes more than before.

"What do you mean, what kind of architect?" I asked, suspecting that he was testing me.

"Do you wish to be one of these second-handers who design from a computer and turn the courses out like machine parts? Or do you want to be an architect with artistic flair and interesting but rational ideas?"

"Well, I sort of believe that if I work hard to create thoughtful holes, that the business side will take care of itself," I replied, repeating out loud the words I had said so often to myself.

MacKenzie smiled. "I used to think the same thing! But I spent too much of my own money and never charged enough...well, that's another story," he said, waving the thought away with his hand.

However, I wanted to hear about that. "You went broke?" I prodded.

"Just about. I had trouble tracking down some fees during the Depression years. However, I have no regrets. What makes me angry is what has been done to some of my original courses. I worked bloody damn hard to document them with photographs and maps, but those foolish green committees still thought they knew better and changed them. The cowards all waited until they thought I was dead, though. Little do they know!"

"I've always wondered what you thought of some of the alterations made to your designs," I said.

"Well, I don't mind changes such as those that have transpired here at The Valley Club. Bunkers evolve, and some have to be abandoned during tough times such as the Second World War. Here, they are gently bringing back the old look of the course, though I am proud to say it has never lost its playing satisfaction for the members. But the cry of freakishness has been raised at some of my other designs where they've added lakes and bunkers and planted way too many trees — that irritates the hell out of me!"

I stared straight ahead in silence as the old man stopped the cart just behind the fifth green under the shade of an old oak.

"I always obtained finality in the construction of my courses, and it is as much of an affront to me as an architect to sabotage my work as it would be to an artist to alter one of his paintings."

"Do you think green committees are still a problem?"

"Worse than ever!" he snapped. "The world has been overtaken by backward, irrational and irresponsible committees!"

I stared at him, hoping to hear more. Apparently though, he had pledged to himself not to talk about such things. I thought if I could out-silence him just a little longer, the old man couldn't resist the temptation to hold forth on one of his favorite topics. I was right.

"Don't get me wrong, I am all for the democratic process," he said. "But I just don't comprehend why society has become so obsessed with pleasing everyone, including those who'll never be satisfied? You can not please everyone, and when you try to, it is done at the expense of art, music, politics, or whatever is the matter at hand."

"But you always talk about building golf courses with the first principle being that you build with the greatest good for the greatest number of players in mind," I reminded him.

"That is different." MacKenzie explained. "I said that because golf holes in my day were being built with only the championship player in mind, and the average man was being forgotten. Today, it has come full circle. Your society demands correctness for all. The result is that ideas and principles that have proven successful are being ignored in order to achieve perfect fairness for all. I believed in creating interest for all. There is no good, honest skill demanded of anyone anymore."

I thought he was referring to political correctness, but I wasn't sure.

"There is an old Persian saying," he said, getting back to committees and ignorance in general. "He who knows not, and knows not that he knows not, is a fool. Avoid him.

"He who knows not, and knows that he knows not, will learn. Teach him.

"He who knows, and knows not that he knows, will fail. Pity him.

"He who knows, and knows that he knows, is a wise man. Follow him."

A foursome in two golf carts drove by and waved at us as they were headed for the Valley Club's sixth tee.

"Bloody worst thing I have ever seen," the old man snorted from the seat of his own cart. "Will you look at that? Four healthy young men driving around in buggies for four hours on a pleasurable walking course. I used to advocate golf for health reasons, but now the walking aspect of the game is disappearing and caddies are almost nonexistent. Who would have ever figured on that?"

"But, you are using a cart right now," I pointed out.

"I never said I didn't think these buggies were a wonderful thing for old men like me who can still get out and play a few holes thanks to a cart. It's the young people who should not rely on them. There are courses that require you to take a cart and then keep you relegated to the paths. That isn't golf!"

The old Scot collected himself for a moment.

"Now, Johnny, let me ask. Are you willing to quit your comfortable little job?"

"For what?"

"To come work with me, of course."

I laughed, stunned and unsure what to say. "Doing what exactly?"

"I need a young man like you. I'm behind the times when it comes to technical issues, and I just don't have the resolve to spend time in the field like I used to. In return, I'll teach you everything I know about golf and life. If you listen to me, I can make you the greatest golf architect in the world."

This guy had a lot of nerve, that was for sure. But it was hard to resist what he was offering. "Well...where would we work out of?" I asked.

"We don't need an opulent office. We will move to the site where our first project will be built."

I was still skeptical. "Do you have some money to start a business and pay me? I need to make a living."

"Things will be a bit lean at first, but I think we'll manage. I can do one of those book signings to generate a little attention."

"You can't do a book signing!" I laughed. "You're infamous for not putting up with dumb questions without offending people!"

The old man glared at me. But there was just enough doubt in his eyes that I knew I'd made my point.

"I'll try my best," he promised. "But you have to understand, I come from a time when society believed in its experts, and the experts were more than just good public relations men. During my heyday, authorities in various fields were trusted to do their work. Nowadays, everyone thinks he is an expert on everything, when in reality they aren't experts on anything!"

I shook my head. "You can't go into a design project with that attitude. You haven't got a chance with a client," I said. But I knew that MacKenzie was right. I had watched Bill concede to ridiculous demands by developers on a daily basis just so he would not lose work, which was sad, considering clients were paying for his expertise, or at least, his perceived expertise.

"Are you with me or not?" the old fellow demanded impatiently. "I promise it will be worth your while. You were probably going to quit that job soon anyway, and you have some money saved up. Haven't you?"

I was stunned. "How did you know I was thinking about quitting? And how did you find me?"

"I know these things," the Doctor smiled. "I still have some connections, and actually, you were recommended to me by Alex McDonald. Now, is it MacKenzie and Grant, Incorporated?"

I wanted to believe in him. I wanted it to be true. But part of me was still suspicious.

"Why me?" I asked. "With your name, you could do this on your own just fine"

"No," he said. "I've done my research, but I need your youth and energy on my side."

"So, you just want someone to be a front man for you?" I guessed.

"*No!*" MacKenzie roared. "I'm looking for someone with more than just youth."

"Well, what then?"

"Spiritual integrity."

I blinked. I was honored, and speechless. Alister MacKenzie thought I had spiritual integrity. How could I turn him down? My family would think I'd lost my mind. On the other hand, life was too short to keep churning out shabby golf courses.

"Are you with me?" the old man asked again. "If this does not work to your liking, you can always go back to your miserable old job turning out second-hand rubbish."

I looked straight into his old eyes. This was the first time I had been presented with the opportunity to take a real risk in life. Everything had always been so programmed. High school. College. Degree. Job. New car. Nice apartment. Promotion.

"What do I tell Bill Mario?"

He laughed. "I'm sure you'll think of something!"

I had run out of questions. I had never been so confused in my life. But somehow it seemed like the right thing to do. It's a good thing to be scared and unsure sometimes, isn't it? Besides, how could I lose?

"I'm not getting any younger!" the gruff Scot complained, growing impatient.

This really was MacKenzie. How weird. The greatest architect ever, alive and well. "All right! I'll do it."

With that we shook hands, and only later that day did it really hit me that I was going to be working with a man who had had Bobby Jones, Perry Maxwell, Chandler Egan and Robert Hunter among his list of past associates.

*D*octor MacKenzie drove me around the northeastern side of The Valley Club of Montecito, explaining his thoughts on each hole and telling stories about some of the problems that had come up during construction. He told me tales of Robert Hunter and the founders of the Valley Club. Having succumbed to the fact that this was MacKenzie, I just sat and listened in awe.

While he drove me around the course telling more stories, I drifted off. Who was going to believe this? Would people think I had flipped out? But imagine what kind of work we could get with MacKenzie's name! That was, if anyone would believe us.

5

"We need a *real* office — this won't cut it," I rudely announced as we stood in the doorway of The Valley Club maintenance yard, looking at the small, vanilla-walled office inside.

MacKenzie glanced apologetically at Alex McDonald. "Johnny, do you have to insult my friend here?"

Thankfully, McDonald was a businessman. "Don't worry, Mac, besides, John has a point," Alex said. "This is why I recommended him to you — if you two are going to make a dent in the architecture business you need a real office with phones, a fax and a computer."

MacKenzie reddened as he tapped his foot on the linoleum floor, lighting a cigarette to help burn off his frustration. The foot tapping was even more intrusive because he was wearing the big-soled leather bucks that the major fashion designers had recently brought back into style. Only his were originals from the '20s!

"All I want is a bloody sketch pad, a desk, and the address of the nearest postal office!" MacKenzie declared.

"But Doctor," I reminded him, "people are going to be calling and faxing us proposals."

"This will do just fine. Understand?" MacKenzie said, delivering that penetrating stare he was known to give unsuspecting folk like me from time to time. Over lunch later in the day, we agreed to set up shop at the Valley Club until a project came along. Mac promised he'd reevaluate the office situation later on. For some reason I sensed that he was not in this for the long haul. I had to remember he *was* 128.

$\mathcal{W}$e spent Sunday sitting in a golf cart at the Valley Club driving around the course, getting acquainted, talking about life and, most of all, discussing what our goals would be if a project came along. All things considered, it went well and I was surprised how comfortable I was around a man I had worshipped through my research and reading.

The Doctor did get upset a few times when I wouldn't express my opinions. It was just my habit not to say much around my elders or employers, and it certainly wasn't any easier around a gruff old Scot. Alister MacKenzie was not a man you could exactly cozy up to, but I did sense that perhaps he had learned to relax a little bit over the years.

On Monday, we dropped off the Mario Design bid and plans in San Luis Obispo. MacKenzie joined me for the long car ride and spent the entire trip fidgeting with the power windows and the CD player. The Doctor complained about having to listen to my selection of CDs, though he seemed to finally find one he could tolerate in Fleetwood Mac's mega-selling *Rumours*. But he wanted it turned off when he started analyzing the lyrics of *Go Your Own Way*. The only thing I could figure was that it was bringing back bitter memories of his split with H.S. Colt!

"What the hell is this?" Dr. MacKenzie asked. He held up a folder that stated the cost of hiring Mario Golf Course Design and a hole-by-hole description of Mario's golf course plans for Pigeon Run, complete with Bill's declaration that there "would be no signature holes at Pigeon Run — just a signature course."

"I suppose he thinks his signature means something," the Doctor sniffed. "And what are these pretty little pictures of? They bear a very slight resemblance to what could be construed as golf holes. Nightmarish looking ones at that."

"Those are Bill's drawings for the holes at Pigeon Run," I said.

"Look at this nonsense!" MacKenzie exclaimed, outraged. "There is no thought or strategy behind these holes! The bunkers are merely there to penalize instead of promote thoughtful play. Who drew these?"

I came clean.

"Maybe you could get a straighter, more stale look next time with a little less artistic flair," MacKenzie suggested sarcastically, referring to the polished plans that contained thick and very straight lines. The plans were a far cry from the irregular, soft-edged drawing style that prevailed during the Doctor's active years.

I made a feeble attempt to defend my work. "That is the preferred drawing style today," I said.

"Well, if you're going to present them this way, the least you could do is sneak a little strategy into these holes," he said.

"Bill has not exactly been known for his strategic design work in the last few years," I noted wryly.

"But *your* name is on these sket...or, shall we say, bad drawings," MacKenzie pointed out.

"Well, yes, but, uh...he made me take them right off the computer," I stammered.

"That is no excuse," MacKenzie said flatly. "You can't put your name on this rubbish."

I smiled. "I guess I won't have that problem after I quit today."

Subsequent to dropping off the proposal for Pigeon Run, I telephoned the office and asked for Bill's voice mail. I decided to announce my resignation without the annoying prospect of a live person on the other end of the line who might ask a silly question, such as, "Why are you leaving?"

After I hung up the phone, I felt a sort of perverse satisfaction that I had never felt before. "If only Bill knew he had been dropped for the good Doctor Alister MacKenzie," I thought to myself. Then again, Bill couldn't care less if I left him for Alister MacKenzie or Alistair Cooke.

As much as I wanted to tell Bill why I quit, I made up a story about a family illness and needing to move back to Northern California. I also assured Bill that everything had been safely submitted on time at Pigeon Run and that he could send my final paycheck and office belongings to my home address.

Arrangements were made for me to stay in one of the Valley Club's private cabins overlooking the club driving range and, in the distance, the Pacific Ocean. Dr. MacKenzie had been living in the other cabin for some time.

I returned to the cabins late Monday evening after retrieving some clothes and other personal belongings from my Los Angeles apartment, including copies of Dr. MacKenzie's two books that I wanted him to autograph.

As the sun set behind Santa Barbara Channel, a typical June fog drifted across the Valley Club bringing with it the familiar salty smell of the Pacific. I joined MacKenzie on the porch of his cabin, and we plotted strategy for our leap into the architecture business. The Doctor reported that he had called his stepgrandson, Raymund, who in turn referred him to the publisher of *The Spirit of St. Andrews*. MacKenzie called him, prepared to commit to some book signings.

"What happened?" I asked, amused at the potential response.

"He fainted," MacKenzie chuckled.

"I'll bet."

"They revived him eventually, though."

"How did you convince him that you were who you said you were?"

"I faxed him a handwritten letter and told him some things about the different versions of *The Spirit of St. Andrews* that only a few people know. That fax is quite a pleasurable device. I'm looking forward to sending out some more letters on it."

"Promise me you won't get too comfortable with it," I pleaded. "People these days don't respond well to nasty letters."

"What makes you think I'd send nasty letters?" MacKenzie asked, fighting a smile. "So cynical are the youth today!"

I let him know that I had done my research. "Do I need to remind you about some of the articles and letters you wrote over the years?"

"I've no idea what you mean!" MacKenzie pleaded in mock innocence, losing the battle with his smile.

"Do the names Joshua Crane and Gene Sarazen ring a bell?" I asked, proud of my hours of research at the Ralph W. Miller Golf Library in Southern California. During MacKenzie's heyday he had several exchanges with a *Golf Illustrated* writer named Joshua Crane over the merits of the Old Course and Crane's numerical rating system for famous courses. After several nasty exchanges, MacKenzie finally told Crane to turn his rankings upside down if he wanted to be accurate!

Sarazen and MacKenzie had feuded on several subjects, most notably MacKenzie's design work at Troon's Portland Course. Sarazen was bitter about failing to qualify for the British Open there. MacKenzie also had called Sarazen a "vandal," in response to Sarazen's suggestion that the cup be enlarged to make putting easier.

"Sarazen is alive and well, I understand," MacKenzie said casually.

I sent him a warning look. "Don't even think about faxing him a letter," I said.

"Oh, but it would be fun, would it not?" MacKenzie smiled, rubbing his old hands together.

"The man is in his nineties," I said. "You could kill him."

"I'm almost 130!" the Doctor exclaimed. "Don't tell me about being old."

"I'm sorry, I keep forgetting...because you don't look a day over 110," I teased.

"Relax, Johnny. I'm here to improve modern golf and its course architecture. Not to convince an irrational man like Sarazen of the value of my work. A golf architect must not be unduly influenced by hostile criticism, but should give most sympathetic consideration to criticism of a constructive nature. Our friend Mr. Sarazen could always visualize only his own game. He got his wish to see Augusta altered to fit his style, even if it was long after his playing days were over. I see the same selfish attitude among some of your professional golfers today. Amazingly, it seems every one of them is a practicing architect on the side! Thank the Lord that Sarazen didn't go into the business!"

"Player–architects, we call them," I explained wryly. "Bill Mario has worked with a total of four so far."

"I'll tell you why I have a problem with most professional players who think they are qualified to design a golf course," MacKenzie said. He paused to collect his thoughts. Then he moistened his throat with a shot of scotch from a glass that sat conveniently next to his wooden patio chair.

"A golf architect must have a sporting instinct," he began. "If he has had training in many and varied branches of sport and has analyzed the characteristics that provide a maximum of pleasurable excitement in them, so much the better. However, it is essential that he disregard his own game entirely and look upon all design work in a purely impersonal manner. He should be able to put himself in the position of the best player that ever lived and at the same time be sympathetic toward the beginner and high handicap player. Above all, he should be able to come to a prompt decision as to what is the greatest good for the greatest number."

I interrupted. "And you don't think the Tour pros do that?"

"Well, just look at their work! Some of their courses are fine, but most of these professionals haven't the faintest clue what the average man goes through. The courses designed by some of the golf pros suffer from a complete absence of variety, strategy, and interest. These pros work on their games seven days a week to perfect their swing and their touch. Yet, they think if they visit a course for a single day they are qualified to create a layout for players of varying proficiency. It's completely irrational!"

"You've seen some of their courses?" I guessed.

"Oh yes, I have toured several."

"Really? How did you do that without being noticed?"

"I paid to play them. No one knew who I was, and if they suspected, they didn't have the courage to ask! You will see. Just watch at the book signing Friday."

"A book signing? Where?" I asked apprehensively.

"It seems an association of golf course superintendents is having a large convention later this week in a place called Anaheim. Twenty thousand visitors all in one place to study how to manicure these bloody courses to death when a team of rabbits could do just as well! Amazing."

The Doctor was known to exaggerate just a bit from time to time. Personally, I think the Golf Course Superintendents Association of America is one of the best organizations in golf, and there isn't a more important group of people in the game than superintendents. Since MacKenzie probably wasn't current on what the superintendent does these days, I decided to stay out of any argument about rabbits versus greenkeepers, though I must agree that some courses are over-manicured.

"And you are going to sign *The Spirit of St. Andrews* there?" I asked.

"Yes," MacKenzie chuckled. "And we are going to do some 'networking' as your generation likes to call it."

"Where did you hear that phrase?"

"My stepgrandson Raymund provided me with loads of literature. I try to keep abreast of current events, believe it or not."

"But no one will believe it's you!"

"You did."

"That took a lot of convincing, and I had studied your photo and knew your life story," I reminded him.

"I am just going to explain to them that I never died and that I have been in seclusion all of these years and if they can't see that I'm extremely old, then too damn bad."

I didn't have a response.

MacKenzie smiled, picking up the conversation and throwing in a little more Scottish accent than normal. "Ye jist want tae know my secret fer longevity! Dinna even think aboot askin'!"

"But you were supposedly cremated and your ashes dropped from a plane over the Pasatiempo golf course. And wasn't a death certificate signed?"

"Oh come on, Johnny! I'm a doctor. I have connections. Certificates can be forged, and ashes, why you can get those anywhere. Though it nearly killed me when I saw the bill for that staged plane flight over Pasatiempo!"

6

The line of spectators stretched for hundreds of feet outside the massive steel doors of the Anaheim Convention Center. Never in the history of the Golf Course Superintendent's Association of America had an author attracted such a crowd for a book signing. Actually, it was the first time there was any *real* commotion at the convention. Normally a meeting place for twenty thousand superintendents, agronomists, and various golf course suppliers and turf equipment manufacturers, the convention had been transformed into a circus, with television and print reporters converging to lay their eyes on the 128-year-old man who claimed to be Alister MacKenzie.

Before the Doctor appeared for his signing, I walked the aisles and perused the various booths. From time to time I overheard conversations about MacKenzie, with comments ranging from the positive, "I think it's really him," to my initial feeling of, "There's no way it's him!"

I was named as the contact man for Doctor MacKenzie, and it was remarkable how much interest there was in documenting his reappearance. The Golf Channel's Anne Liguori requested a one-hour interview, as did CNN's Jim Huber and ABC's Jimmy Roberts.

I began to realize how unbelievable all of this was when Mike Wallace of *60 Minutes* called, hoping for an exclusive interview. Desperate to be the first, CBS also sent its top sports commentator, Jim Nantz, in hopes of landing the first televised one-on-one conversation with the Doctor.

The age factor alone brought out the tabloid shows from nearby Hollywood, not to mention lucrative offers from all of the major daytime talk shows. I had to decline all interviews because MacKenzie's energy level didn't last more than a few hours, so we had to take things slow. Being the savvy PR guy that I was, I wanted to build anticipation for his reappearance, which now included a speech, so I kept him in hiding.

The hype over MacKenzie's reappearance got so bad that we had to check him into his nearby hotel room under an assumed name. The Doctor considered several clever aliases before settling on that of the famed late 18th century landscape architect from Britain, and one of his major inspirations, Humphrey Repton. The Doctor figured anyone resourceful enough to connect him with that name deserved to get through on the telephone. No one was.

"I want to tell you an old caddie story that I remember from my days at St. Andrews," Doctor MacKenzie began, addressing a standing-room-only crowd of at least four thousand, as flashbulbs exploded every time he made even the slightest gesture. Even though he hadn't faced a crowd in years, MacKenzie proved to be a natural speaker, sitting comfortably in a large chair with a microphone strategically positioned in front of him.

The Doctor was dressed in his usual beige plus-four suit and vest, though today he had added a particularly powerful-looking burgundy tie for his lecture. He spoke from prepared notes, gesturing occasionally and sipping water from a glass sitting on a small table at his right. No one else sat on the dais.

"There was a very silent and focused old caddie at the Old Course named John Lorrie," the Doctor continued, telling a story like only a Scot can. "So one day, while carrying for his usual client, a University Professor, the two were at the Heather hole coming in. Ol' Johnny saw in the distance a well known and admirable golfer — to whom the game is a serious business — looking disconsolate and almost miserable. He was disabled, and by this time could only walk out to the Old Course to watch the matches of others.

"'Well,' the Professor remarked to his caddie, 'Mr. Robertson is surely very ill; he looks as if his life-work were gone.'

"'Aye, sir,' replied the caddie, 'You see he's one of them that has nothing else to do. Poor things, I pity them. It's a grand thing, sir, to have a *profession*, like you and me."

The room erupted in laughter.

"There's a point to this story, as I hope you will see," the Doctor said. "As greenkeepers, many of you men know how it feels when your profession is not respected. Imagine what those old caddies go through — they are taunted and laughed at, yet they take their job oh so seriously, and they're passionate about what they do. But having the benefit of 128 years under my belt, I am sad to tell you that I don't see this kind of passion respected or encouraged as it was in my day. In particular, I am referring to the once artistic profession of golf course architecture."

MacKenzie paused for effect before proceeding. I noticed he was a much different man when addressing a crowd. Perhaps he was nervous, but he seemed to be talking more formally and much faster.

"There are many qualities required for the making of a successful person," he continued. "The job of the golf architect is no different than that of any other position of responsibility. It is such a powerful thing to toy with nature — a power that I see being misused today by those practicing the profession," said MacKenzie.

"The training of the golf architect is purely mental, not physical. The architect's playing ability, should it be poor to average, should not prevent him from being a successful designer of courses, just as being an expert player does not ensure one's ability as a teacher of new students to the game. In the case of the architect, or the teacher or even the good greenkeeper, he must have imagination. That is essential to success in any profession.

"The architect's knowledge of the game should be so intimate that he knows instinctively what is likely to produce good golf and good golfers. He must have more than a passing acquaintance with the best courses and the best golfing holes. He should not only study them and analyze the features that make them what they are, but he must have a sense of proportion.

"Sadly, I have frequently seen large sums of money wasted in your modern designs in a futile attempt to make every hole visually perfect or to eliminate blind shots. It requires the expenditure of literally millions of dollars to achieve this most imperfect of perfections. And do you know who pays for these enormous construction bills in the long run? The dues-paying member or the green fee–paying customer."

MacKenzie lifted a copy of *The Spirit of St. Andrews* and held it up before the crowd, much to the satisfaction of its publisher, who had announced earlier in the day that an updated version of the book, featuring an new afterword by the Doctor, would be in stores by the fall.

"In this book, which I am sure you all will purchase today," MacKenzie grinned, "I predicted that future designers would be likely to achieve more perfect results and make fuller use of all the natural features because they would have access to more up-to-date methods. I wrote that in 1932. It has turned out that I was, most uncharacteristically, incorrect!"

A nervous buzz spread through the crowd of superintendents, product salesmen, course construction company CEOs and architects. They were probably bracing for what might be coming next. The ones squirming in their seats had to be the architects.

"The society I see today," Mac said with a note of disappointment, "has so many more technical and informational advantages than the one I worked in, yet I see these resources wasted and misused. Golf, particularly course construction, provides perfect examples of this sad phenomenon today. Your society is so obsessed with statistics and labeling artistic endeavors with numbers, that creativity and originality are frowned upon out of fear, and golf courses are simply mass-produced with no artistic flair whatsoever.

"I am, of course, referring to the massive amount of earthmoving that occurs today in the building of a golf course. Sure, there are sites that need to be rearranged for golf to even be played on them. But Mother Nature put bumps and hills and canyons on this earth for a reason, and many wonderful courses have been created while accommodating those features. Leveling them and creating something artificial in appearance is not the answer. But I know why the architects do it — the average golfer today wants his hand held like a little child. He wants every hole to be simple and right in front of him, with nothing out of the ordinary to disturb his mind. But the golfer today is missing out on the charm, mystery and excitement of playing an occasional blind shot, or of experiencing a unique and natural hole."

The Doctor continued to get more specific. "Does the average player really know what he likes? One often hears a player express totally divergent opinions about a particular hole or course. When he plays it successfully, it is a wonderful hole, and when he plays it poorly it is a terrible hole. It is largely a question of the spirit in which the game is played. Does the player look upon it from the 'card and pencil' point of view and condemn anything that has disturbed his steady series of threes and fours, or does he approach each hole in the spirit of the true sportsman?"

MacKenzie sipped some water before switching subjects.

"A perfect example of your society's fascination with numbers is the disturbing trend I see in championship golf today, where the primary method of competitive play is stroke play, as opposed to match play. When every stroke matters in a round, as it does in stroke play, the game requires less mental skill, and places too much importance on physical agility. The stroke play mentality also breeds the kind of golfers who will inevitably complain about every hollow, brown spot, or unraked bunker that threatens their final score. They acquire the "green grass" mentality, as well as other ridiculous expectations for course maintenance where promoting fairness takes priority over all other matters."

The superintendents in the audience applauded. They, after all, were the ones who always took the blame for every hollow or brown spot, and they are the ones who are denounced when something unfair happens to the golfers who play their courses.

"The beauty of match play is really quite simple," the Doctor continued. "In match play, the player has to deal with his opponent on each hole, and *only* the final score of each hole is of any importance, thus reducing complaints about bad luck when a player plays well but has high scores on one or two holes."

Applause erupted again from the superintendents, who had sat through many committee meetings during which members recounted dismal stories about bad bounces off the hard spot in the eleventh fairway, or the mud puddle on number two that prevented them from breaking 90 for the first time.

"This mentality seems to have crept into the minds of most of the golf architects," MacKenzie continued. "Many poor and downright dull courses have been made in the last sixty years in a futile attempt to eliminate the element of luck. You can no more eliminate luck in golf than you can in any sport or in life. You can't punish every bad golf shot, and you can't create situations where complete fairness is assured. If you succeeded you would only make the game, and life, uninteresting."

The crowd murmured in agreement. Encouraged, the Doctor continued.

"The greatest decline I see in the game today, which I blame on the architects, is the lack of thought put into the placement of hazards on your courses," MacKenzie continued, pressing his lips together as if he had just tasted cheap scotch. "Hazards should be placed with a purpose in mind, and each one should have *some* influence on the line of play to the hole. My experience with today's courses is one of despair and disbelief. I can't tell you how many bunkers I have seen placed to catch shots that are already wayward and in serious trouble for the next play. Hazards should be placed strategically to disrupt the line of play and force the golfer to think about the alternatives open to him. That is what Bob Jones and I did at Augusta. We built only twenty-two bunkers in all, yet each hole had several interesting features for every level of golfer."

The Doctor then expanded his discussion of hazard placement to include major tournament setup conditions. "I am even more disturbed by the trend toward narrowing fairways and growing five-inch rough just off the sides," he continued. "This may come as a surprise to some of you, but I find that rough grass is of little interest as a hazard. Sadly, I see that rough is considered a desirable hazard in American golf. It is frequently much more difficult to play from than a fearsome looking bunker, it causes considerable annoyance in lost balls, and no one ever gets the same thrill driving over a stretch of rough as he does over a fearsome-looking bunker.

"This craze clearly started because of your national championship, and you even see this 'narrow fairway, high rough' mentality permeating the Open Championship overseas nowadays. I never thought I'd see the day when they would install irrigation on the great links of the British Isles. It amazes me that the governing bodies of the game have decided that narrow fairways are an adequate method for crowning national champions. And now I see they mow fairways with walk-behind mowers as well! Television coverage of professional tournaments has given green committees the impression that this is how all golf course conditions should be all the time. This could not be more false."

MacKenzie paused before finishing his point. Several men in the audience were shaking their heads in disagreement, which only encouraged MacKenzie.

"Narrow fairways bordered by long grass make bad golfers!" the Doctor declared flatly. "And narrow fairways destroy the harmony and continuity of the game, causing a stilted and cramped style, destroying all freedom of play and creative shotmaking. And isn't that the real joy of the game? Creating shots and making bold recovery plays?"

A smattering of applause came from the audience. I sensed they were ready to move on to another topic, but the Doctor wanted to finish making his point.

"I always tell committees that fairways should gradually widen where the long drive goes. In this way a long driver is given a little more latitude for pulling or slicing. I see exactly the opposite happening in your major championships. For some reason, those running the tournaments want to discourage the long hitter, perhaps because not enough has been done to regulate the golf ball and equipment, or perhaps out of some sort of perverse envy that they themselves can't hit the ball long distances. Either way, rough grass is of no value for protecting danger points; it has no effect in keeping people straight...it merely prolongs the length of time players are in the danger zone and the length of time it takes to play. In my day we could play three rounds before dinner; now you can barely finish one round in a day!"

MacKenzie's critical comments on rough drew a surprisingly big cheer from the audience. Perhaps Mac's point was finally getting across.

The Doctor then turned his wrath on trees. First, he expressed wonder at the number of trees he saw planted on courses.

"Before I address the topic of trees, please understand that I love trees. They are beautiful, often amazing and a wonderful component of nature. With that said, you must understand that fairways bordered by straight lines of trees are not only inartistic, but they produce tedious and uninteresting golf. Many green committees have ruined my handiwork by planting trees like rows of soldiers along the borders of the fairways and turning once beautiful properties into jungles. I do not know exactly why this is, but I see that it is more prevalent today than ever before. My particular favorite is the memorial tree planted each time a member passes on. Cemeteries are built to memorialize; golf courses are for pleasurable exercise!"

MacKenzie switched topics again, seemingly building toward his conclusion. This time, he referred to the loss of interesting and skillful approach shots to greens.

"Soft turf and multiple-tiered elevated greens discourage everything but an aerial attack on the hole. It takes far more skill to hit an approach shot to a green on the ground. Any sixteen handicapper can play a pitch shot, but few of even the best players can play a run-up shot. Bobby Jones did not appreciate the Old Course at St. Andrews until he had learned to play this shot. Any course that merely caters to an everlasting pitch at every hole can never be entirely satisfactory."

Then the Doctor turned his frustration toward modern golf architects — the crescendo he seemed to be building toward in his speech.

"I am most troubled by some of the current practicing golf architects, and note that I said *some*."

MacKenzie paused. "I do not claim that the game has been completely void of architectural or technological progress since the 1920s, or that golf course design should adhere strictly to the principles of my generation."

I looked down at my notes, praying that the Doctor would not mention Bill Mario by name.

"However...to be original, and to expand on the work of the fine architects who practiced in my day, you have to understand why we did what we did," he continued. "I will go so far as to say that the work I have seen from many architects indicates that they have failed to study and understand what creates an interesting hole and what made certain early architects successful. Once an architect studies and comprehends what my generation accomplished, then he will be able to build on those basic principles and create original, interesting designs for all golfers. But until that kind of study occurs, you will continue to see dull and insipidly designed courses dotting the landscapes of America.

"Golf architecture is an art closely allied to that of the artist or sculptor, but also requiring a scientific knowledge of many other subjects. Unfortunately, most of the modern design work is so consumed with the scientific side that any artistry, subtlety or character have been lost. The result will be a generation of courses that will be seen for what they really are: expanses of green grass, trees and water, intended merely for socking the ball around and nothing else."

Now clearly captivated by MacKenzie, the audience sat perfectly still. Then he made his move. He was about to change the business of golf course design.

"As of today, I am declaring myself available to design one, or perhaps two golf course projects in the next year. I plan to show the world again what it means to build a masterpiece."

After the initial collective gasp from the crowd, the room hummed with speculation, and then a thundering applause finally erupted. The thought of the architect who designed Cypress Point and Augusta National possibly giving us one more brilliant creation had finally sunk in.

"My associate, John Grant, who is seated here in the front, and I are forming MacKenzie and Grant, Golf Course Architects. We welcome the opportunity to restore some of my old courses, or accept a new project, though I can't promise we will be available for more than one project at this point."

I felt like the whole room was staring at me. As MacKenzie assessed the stunned crowd's reaction, he glanced over to me and, for the first time since meeting him, I felt an enormous burden being placed on my shoulders. He gave me a quick nod, notifying me to brace myself for a barrage of requests — the lecture was about to end.

"Thank you for joining me today," the Doctor finished with a smile. "If you should have any other questions about my philosophy, I think you will find the answers in *The Spirit of St. Andrews*. Thank you for your time, and may you all be blessed with fine growing conditions and unobtrusive green committees!"

7

The Doctor and I met in his room at the Hilton after the book signing. I estimated that he had signed well over a thousand copies of *The Spirit of St. Andrews*, so when we returned to the hotel I poured him a big glass of scotch. While he savored his restorative, I sat down and made notes covering the various appointments I had scheduled concerning potential work. The Doctor phoned in a food order.

He had handled the book buyers pretty well until about book number five hundred. The cranky and gruff side started to emerge after a few too many questions like, "What do you think of Tiger Woods?" or "How do we redesign our home course to accommodate Tiger Woods?"

Fortunately, someone sneaked the Doctor some scotch in a can of cola, and he sailed through the remaining books, though he wasn't too fond of posing for cameras with flashes. He was particularly annoyed with the few patrons who called him "Doc" and put their arms around him as if he were a long lost golfing buddy.

While MacKenzie signed books, I pulled up a chair and listened to offers. I don't think I realized how important the Doctor's return was, until I saw the reactions of those approaching me about work. Since most of the offers were pretty vague, I set up conference calls and gave out the Valley Club address for correspondence.

The first significant offer came from a USGA official. They were interested in talking to MacKenzie about becoming the unofficial "Open Doctor," better known as the architect who comes in and touches up future U.S. Open sites. I thought it seemed like a pretty ridiculous request considering that MacKenzie had just spent half his speech criticizing the U.S. Open course setup style.

Someone from the PGA Tour guaranteed a TPC design contract for the firm of MacKenzie and Grant. Though he did preface his request by declaring that we would probably have to be assisted on the project by a famous player–architect, in order to, as the man put it, "add some name value to the project and ensure that the course design credit will have a Tour presence." I wanted to ask him if he had been working on that line during the entire lecture, but I passed. All I could do was act grateful and laugh to myself at the thought of MacKenzie getting advice from some Tour pro.

An officer from the American Society of Golf Course Architects said Mac would be granted an honorary membership, as did the President of the Golf Course Superintendent's Association. All of the television producers and golf writers returned to me for another shot at signing MacKenzie up for an interview, but I didn't commit him to anything.

I listened sympathetically to several superintendents who had to deal with nightmarish green committees that they hoped only the gruff MacKenzie could deal with. Most of their courses were in odd places or lacked much architectural merit, but I kindly took down names and numbers and promised to get back to them at a later date.

Another man with an almost indiscernible British accent claimed to be a high-ranking member of the Royal and Ancient Golf Club of St. Andrews. He invited the Doctor to return to St. Andrews to receive an honorary membership in the Royal and Ancient, an honor that is rarely granted. I took the man's card and promised that I would pass along the message, knowing that was one offer MacKenzie would want to accept.

Several wealthy developers approached with million dollar offers and sites they described in one of two ways. Either it was the
"Pebble Beach" of their state — meaning there was a natural body
of water within five miles of the site. Or worse, the development
was the "Augusta National" of their town — meaning it would be
an ultra-private club created by a group of CEOs who couldn't get
into the real Augusta.

The only enticing offer came midway through MacKenzie's
book signing. After I had heard most of the initial requests, a tall,
well-dressed man walked up to me. "I'm Bob Jensen, the golf course
superintendent at Augusta National Golf Club," the man said.

"Uh-oh," I thought to myself. This could get peculiar. There
was virtually nothing left of the Doctor's original design at Augusta other than the routing and a couple of bunkers.

"Do you think Dr. MacKenzie would be interested in a visit to
see the course?" he asked.

I paused before uncharacteristically blurting out, "Well, it has
sort of been stripped of any resemblance of his original design, at
least from what I have seen."

"Yes, I know that," the man answered pleasantly. Either he was
unshaken by my insult, or he kept his thoughts that I was a snot-
nosed punk to himself. After a brief pause, the man continued. "I
think Dr. MacKenzie might understand some of the changes, considering how prominent the Masters has become these days."

Though I had never discussed it with MacKenzie, I was certain the Doctor would *not* understand the changes and would ver-
bally demolish the club for the alterations that had been made to
his design. Even though the course has evolved very nicely, and
many of the concepts he and Bob Jones preached in the beginning
are still practiced, no architect likes to see his work altered. I also
suspected that MacKenzie would take issue with Augusta's excessive maintenance practices, which set a poor example for the millions of golfers watching on television.

"I will speak to him about a visit. May I have him call you?" I said, in my best imitation of a well-mannered secretary.

"Please do," he replied, writing his hotel room number on the back of his card. "Let's keep it discreet, though. You know how the media tend to make a big deal about anything relating to Augusta."

"So, Johnny, what have we got?" MacKenzie asked. He was sitting on the foot of his bed, still dressed in his plus-fours, cutting into a New York rib eye steak.

"We need to talk about that, Doctor," I said, uninspired by our initial prospects.

"Johnny, we're partners. Tell me what you have," he said. "And it's Mac, please. Now, let's hear it!"

"You've never told me what kind of projects are a high priority," I said. "Resorts, public, private. What?"

"Johnny, I want to prove how inexpensively a good course can be built. I want to work on one last great site. Preferably authentic, sandy linksland and preferably for someone who appreciates our services and who will trust us to build something special."

I sighed. "Oh, boy."

"What is it, son?"

"A project like that is every architect's dream!" I said. "Those kinds of courses and sites don't grow on trees, you know?"

"Yes, I understand, but I've lived this long, and I can hang on long enough to find just one more."

"But I just quit my job, and I need the work," I pointed out. "It's a privilege to hang out with you and learn from you, but I need income."

"Hang out?" he asked, totally ignoring my financial worries.

"You know, traveling with you and working together," I explained.

"That's better," Mac said. "In the future, no more of this California surfer English. So tell me, what were we offered?"

"To be blunt, nothing in the United States that is very interesting. The USGA wants you to be the new 'Open Doctor;' the Tour wants you to design a TPC — probably with some player who claims to love architecture but won't even know who you are; and Augusta National's superintendent invited you down for a tour of what's left of your design."

MacKenzie seemed surprised by the last offer. "Well, what did you tell the Augusta chap?"

"I told him that you might be interested but because they have eliminated virtually all hints of your original design that I wouldn't count on anything."

"Good work, Johnny. Make 'em sweat," Mac said, taking another bite of his steak.

"You have never seen the finished version of Augusta, have you?" I asked.

"Oh, yes, I have," the Doctor said, "I was there just before opening day, though most people don't know that. However, I would like to see it now. I am curious to see how they have corrupted it. I watched a few Masters on television while I was staying with Raymund, so I have some idea of what they've done. It's really quite remarkable."

"Do you think you can control yourself if we visit there?"

"What do you mean, Johnny?"

"You know what I mean," I said. "You can not tell the members that they have spoiled your original design, or that they should stick to their own professions instead of ruining your creation. And you can't ask them if the fool who built the sixteenth green was drunk and blind."

"Why not?" MacKenzie demanded, a smile tugging at the corners of his mouth.

"Because people today don't like to hear candid opinions."

"Too damn bad!" MacKenzie snapped. "I designed that course with Bobby Jones, and we built a damn good test that was certainly suitable to his refined tastes. Besides, isn't freedom of speech one of my rights here in America? Don't I have the right to voice my own opinion?"

"Sure, but I suggest you wait until we leave the Augusta city limits and share them only with me."

"What's the matter? Afraid you won't be invited back to the Masters?" MacKenzie taunted.

"No, dammit!" I growled. "But I hope to have a future in this business, and I don't need the ghost of Clifford Roberts hounding me the rest of my life!"

"Clifford Roberts...what a remarkably difficult man," Mac said with a laugh. "Now, John, relax. By the time we finish a project, you will be able to pick whatever job you want. Trust me."

Finish a project? How about starting one first?

"Now call the man from Augusta, Johnny, and set up a visit for next week," MacKenzie said, interrupting my anxious thoughts. "Tell the gentleman that I look forward to coming, and tell him that I am quite privileged — no, *honored* to be invited to the club. That'll keep 'em guessing!" MacKenzie said with a chuckle, raising his glass in a mock salute.

8

With his outdated plus-fours turning heads in the terminal at Santa Barbara Airport, Doctor MacKenzie and I boarded a chartered jet for Augusta, Georgia. The Club arranged for the flight just to avoid word of Mac's visit to Augusta getting out.

Besides a mysterious bag that was probably full of scotch, Mac brought along a file of paperwork for the trip. Once our pre-dawn flight was off the ground, he opened the file and proceeded to tell me the entire history of the Augusta National Golf Club project, complete with letters, sketches and foldout maps of his first "Augusta National Golf Links" routing. He also had his rendering of the completed 1933 design.

"After the Grand Slam year in 1930, Bob Jones was tired of competitive golfing pressures and retired while he was still the best player in the game," Mac said. "He told me that his retirement plans included continuing his law practice and working on some other ventures he had previously established in Atlanta. The rest of his plan was to create his dream course — a golf club where he could enjoy the game with his friends in a quiet, relaxed setting. Of course, his first step was to find a piece of property in Atlanta."

I had actually read most of this before, but I listened politely because Mac seemed to genuinely enjoy telling the story. It didn't hurt that I was sitting in the plush surroundings of a Gulfstream jet.

"Jones's friend Clifford Roberts, a real nuisance of a man from my perspective, knew of an appealing 365 acres in the town of Augusta where Jones's wife, Mary, was born. The property was called Fruitlands and it belonged to a famous Belgian horticulturist, Prosper Jules Alphonso Berckmans, who had migrated to Augusta in 1857 and planted thousands of trees, azaleas, camellias and other blooming shrubs. Frankly, I wasn't as charmed by the possibilities of a golf course set in the midst of a nursery as Bob was. I was enamored with the property, however, and its varying undulations."

"How did you get the job?" I asked.

"Well, Bob had lost in the first round of the 1929 Amateur at Pebble Beach, so he had some spare time on his hands. He went over and played the course Marion Hollins and I built at Cypress Point. He enjoyed it so much that he accepted Marion's invitation to be at the opening of our new course in Santa Cruz: Pasatiempo. He was even more enamored with what we had done with the inland piece of property at Pasatiempo, and he eventually called me into the Augusta project, much to the chagrin of my competitor those days, old Donald Ross!"

That caught me off guard. "Mr. Ross was considered for the job?"

MacKenzie was laughing. "Of course he was. After all, Ross designed the Augusta Country Club and redesigned East Lake, where Bobby grew up. He was quite prominent in the region, so he expected to land the commission. But I believe Bob Jones wanted someone to collaborate with, and Donald was a stubborn old Scot who didn't have much regard for the opinions of others. So I'm sure he wasn't too pleased when I snatched that commission away from him!"

Well, well. He's referring to someone else as a stubborn Scot?

"How did your design partnership with Mr. Jones work out?" I asked.

"Bob regularly consulted with me during the months of architectural designing," Mac answered. "He rendered assistance of incalculable value. Bob was not only a student of golf, but of golf courses as well. Although I had known him for years, I was amazed at his knowledge and clear recollection of almost all of the most famous golf holes in England and Scotland, as well as America. Bob's college degree in engineering assured that his suggestions were not only unique and original, but practical."

Mac continued. "Bob understood that the first purpose of any golf course should be to give pleasure to the greatest possible number of players, without respect to their capabilities. He believed that each hole should present to each golfer an interesting problem that would test him without being so impossibly difficult that he would have no chance of success. Bob and I were always in agreement that the first principle of every hole we built was that there must be something for the golfer to do, but that something must always be within the realm of reasonable accomplishment."

"Weren't you trying to base many of the holes at Augusta on the principles of famous holes elsewhere?" I asked.

"That is only partly correct," Mac replied. "It has been suggested that it was our intention at Augusta to produce exact copies of the most famous golf holes. But any attempt to do that is doomed to fail. It may be possible to reproduce a famous picture, but the charm of a golf hole may be dependent on a background of sand dunes, trees, or even mountains several miles away. A copy without the surroundings is likely to create an unnatural appearance, causing a feeling of irritation instead of charm. On the other hand, it is advisable to have some knowledge of the world's outstanding holes and to use this knowledge to reproduce some of their most intriguing features, with other traits suggested by the nature of the terrain. That's the concept we had for Augusta."

Near the end of our flight Mac took a nap while I perused his Augusta file. There were some wonderful letters between him and Bob Jones, with updates from Jones on how things were progressing.

There was also the amazing foldout map, dated July 1931. It was Mac's initial routing of Augusta. He originally laid out a par-70 design, including a par-3 19th hole for settling tie matches, and multiple playing routes on each hole. The holes were shown in the order they are in today, with the famed "Amen Corner" as part of the back nine. Sometime before the course opened, the nines were reversed, but it quickly became apparent that the nine including the holes along Rae's Creek made for a better finishing nine, so, soon after the first Masters, the course was switched back to today's configuration.

Mac's file also contained some terse correspondence between him and Clifford Roberts about payment on the remainder of Mac's bill. Evidently Mr. Roberts would not pay the final installment until the course was completed, but Mac tried relentlessly to get his final paycheck. He was definitely low on cash. But who wasn't? It was the middle of the Depression.

The Augusta National Golf Club's superintendent, Bob Jensen, greeted us at the sleepy Augusta airport just outside of town. It was mid-afternoon in Augusta and ridiculously hot. The Doctor wobbled off the Gulfstream having barely awakened from his nap. I was carrying our bags and at the same time trying to guide him to where Jensen's truck awaited.

After Jensen and Mac exchanged pleasantries, we hopped in his air-conditioned Jeep and listened to our itinerary. "Doctor

MacKenzie, you will be meeting our Executive Committee," Jensen said, and I winced. I had been hoping it would only be us and the superintendent, but no such luck.

"What kind of lads are they?" MacKenzie asked innocently.

"They are members at the club — either retired CEOs or prominent executives — who oversee the golf course and other club related matters, and then report to the Chairman," Jensen replied.

"And do they know their place?" MacKenzie wanted to know.

"Uh...What do you mean?" Jensen asked warily.

I interrupted in an attempt to steer the conversation in a safe direction. "What the Doctor means is, do they know something about the architecture of the course?"

"*No*, that's not what I meant," MacKenzie corrected. "I mean, do they know who I am, and do they understand that I'm the expert here?"

"Well, they know that you were the original architect, if that's what you mean," Jensen replied dryly, choosing his words as if he were testifying in front of a Senate subcommittee.

MacKenzie turned to me with a sour look on his face. "Oh, lovely. Did you hear that, Johnny? We've got some more 'experts' to deal with."

"I didn't say that," Jensen said from behind the wheel of his sport utility vehicle. He was turning off the freeway at Washington Boulevard which runs directly in front of the club. The sight before us had to be a shock to MacKenzie. The last time he visited Augusta National, it was the Fruitlands estate in a quiet section of town. Now the main route to the club, Washington Boulevard, had become the world's longest and, some say, ugliest, fast food capital.

Mac spoke again. "I have some idea of what has happened to Augusta National, you know. Just because I've been out of sight for many years doesn't mean I'm out of touch."

"What do you think of the way your design has evolved?" Jensen asked cautiously.

"Oh, you've done some interesting things," MacKenzie allowed, "but most of the changes have come as a result of trends or prevailing fashions, and that is an insult to any self-respecting architect!"

"Fashions?" Jensen asked, bristling a little.

"We've seen cop bunkers come and go," Mac explained. "Then the pot bunkers in straight lines along both sides of the fairway — another backward trend. And of course there was 'alpinization,' when everyone built those horrific-looking mounds."

"What about trends since then?" I interrupted.

"For a time, many of the contemporary designers, like Trent Jones and Wilson, unofficially decreed the total length of the course, or the exact number of one-shot, two-shot and three-shot holes a golf course should have," MacKenzie explained. "Some architects have even dictated that a standard sequence of these holes be set for all courses. That idea goes against the most significant principle in golf course design: variety. No other game has the diversity of playing fields golf has, yet I have seen many courses ruined in an attempt to extend them to so-called 'championship standards.'"

"Well, Augusta has not been lengthened so much as simply altered," I interjected.

"I know that, Johnny. I've seen it on television," the Doctor repeated. "What baffles me is why they thought the original course needed improvement."

Mac had a legitimate gripe, but I was not about to get involved in these discussions, because an argument could be made that Augusta had been improved. Either way, it was going to be a long afternoon.

$\mathcal{B}$ob Jensen looked perplexed as he turned his sport utility vehicle off Washington and waved at the club security guard before driving up Magnolia Lane. Augusta National was closed for the summer so our tour of the course would not be interrupting any golfers.

"I'm not sure exactly what you are saying," Jensen said, trying to clarify the earlier conversation, while I sat in awe of the club's famous entrance drive, Magnolia Lane.

MacKenzie proceeded to hold forth, oblivious to the magnolias. "There is hardly anything new about the ideas of the competent golf architect. If he knows what he is doing, he simply strives to reproduce, and perhaps improve upon, the old ideas as exemplified in the classic, natural courses like St. Andrews."

"I see," Jensen said.

"The other objective of the architect is to place hazards or incorporate existing ones, to give the player as much pleasurable excitement as possible. The evolution of golf reflects much of what is happening in your society today. The architects, just like the politicians, are obsessed with creating fairness for all. The architects have carried it so far that hazards are rarely ever placed for strategic purposes. They seem to be interested in only building them for aesthetic reasons. Thus, the excitement of negotiating them is missing from the game. Not only that, the outrageous improvements in clubs and balls have led to this silly movement to 'protect par,' which I can tell you right now is a prescription for narrow fairways, tall rough and ridiculously penal courses promoting less skill and few or no mental challenges for the golfer."

Mac clearly had not consumed enough alcohol on the flight. He was about as testy as I had ever seen him in our short time together. Thankfully, the end of Magnolia Lane was approaching so I bowed my head and shut my eyes, praying that the visit would not be a complete disaster.

9

"We are thinking of adding some U.S. Open–type rough to slow down Tiger," one committeeman announced, as the group of five members, Bob Jensen, MacKenzie and I congregated outside the clubhouse. My Northern California blood was struggling with the ninety-degree June afternoon, but Mac strode comfortably around in his plus-fours and jacket and tie. He was definitely lending credibility to the perception that old people can never be warm enough.

"Oh that's a splennndid idea," the Doctor responded sarcastically to the committeeman. "That way, in next year's championship Mr. Woods can win by 20 shots instead of 12."

"What makes you think so?" another committeeman asked.

"If you add tall rough grass," Mac explained patiently, "you favor the man who bombs the ball out there 340 yards and hits a lofted short iron club to the green, instead of having to use a club with less loft, which is appreciably more difficult to hit accurately out of the rough."

"But rough should take the driver out of his hands and make the course play longer," Jensen, the superintendent, observed, trying to defend his members.

"Oh, great, so you want the Masters to be a straight driving contest instead of a test of shotmaking and skill!" MacKenzie growled. "Certain kinds of difficulties are needed in our courses to make the game interesting and pleasurable. However, things like man-made rough should be eliminated entirely from the game. Into this class, I think, you can include narrow fairways and excessive numbers of trees."

The Committee members looked at each other. I could read their minds: "See, Cliff Roberts was right. He really is just a grouchy old Scot."

MacKenzie continued addressing the members, who were now standing under the large tree by the Club's glorious veranda. "The annoyance and irritation caused by searching for lost balls and the disturbance of the harmony and continuity of the game are negative factors brought on by narrow fairways and rough, as is the consequent loss of freedom of swing. The result is the production of bad players and fluke winners of golf tournaments."

Another committeeman spoke up in a deep Southern drawl. "But how're we supposed to make the game challengin' for these Tour boys?"

MacKenzie turned to me instead of answering the Augusta member. "Johnny, why is your generation always seeking ways to punish the professional players instead of creating a fine course and letting the conditions and other variables, such as the weather, dictate the final outcome? Is everyone obsessed with preventing skillful play and good scores?"

I didn't answer.

"Oh, stop worrying about your precious career," MacKenzie said in a low-voiced aside to me before returning his gaze to the group.

"Look, gentlemen," Mac continued, "the difficulties that make a hole really interesting are usually those in which a great advantage can be gained by successfully accomplishing heroic carries over hazards or by taking great risks to place a shot so as to gain a big advantage for the next shot. Successfully carrying or skirting a bunker of an alarming or impressive appearance is always a source of satisfaction to the golfer, and yet it is hazards of this description that so often give rise to criticism from the unsuccessful player. Rough, narrow fairways, and more trees will not achieve your purpose, nor will it define a Masters champion. And I'm sure that Bob Jones, God bless him, would agree with me if he were here today."

Despite MacKenzie's pointed lecture, the Committee seemed to take the Doctor's criticism calmly. Maybe they had tuned him out, or perhaps they were more knowledgeable about architecture than MacKenzie gave them credit for. It also seemed that they were prepared to listen to the old man vent his frustration over seeing his original design changed.

After our introductions and Mac's initial tirade, we strolled over to a row of waiting golf carts. Two by two, everyone hopped into a golf cart, with MacKenzie opting to sit with Bob Jensen. I had my own E-Z-GO.

"Now what in the good Lord's name made you give these bunkers the appearance of big white eggs?" MacKenzie asked, as he stepped up to the third tee box, and stared at an arrangement of bunkers that had been added to his original bunker in the landing zone. "Besides the fact that you have added hazards where the keen player needs to approach the green under certain conditions, these bunkers are unsightly, unnatural, and downright ugly. That damned white sand could blind a man."

I had to chuckle under my breath at that one. The committee members offered no defense.

We continued touring the front nine, stopping our carts at each tee and examining each green. MacKenzie noted with satisfaction the relatively unchanged look of numbers four and five, but he felt that the "Redan" nature of his original design on the par-3 sixth had been lost. He stared in silence at the seventh, which had seen drastic alterations. The green once sat on the same level as the fairway, with a green complex modeled after the eighteenth at the Old Course at St. Andrews. The putting surface had been pushed back and heavily bunkered after Byron Nelson drove the green in the 1930s.

The Doctor complemented the committee on the restoration of the hillock-surrounded eighth green. MacKenzie and Jones's original green had changed over the years, and the club had asked Byron Nelson and Joe Finger to restore it to the original design in the '60s.

Our caravan of carts drove all the way through the downhill, par-4 ninth and parked by the putting surface.

"This green has no character, and frankly, is unfair," MacKenzie declared from the hill behind the ninth green. "This used to be a beautiful boomerang-shaped design, which was certainly more challenging and unusual than this dull concoction."

I had to agree with the Doc in this instance. In recent years, balls could be putted off the ninth green and right down the hill below the green. Several old photos had surfaced showing a far more interesting green than the current ninth. I wondered whether

Mac's criticism would damage or enhance its chances of being restored. Based on the reaction of the committee, it wasn't even a consideration.

After we had toured the first nine holes, I was amazed by the behavior of the six committeemen and their superintendent. Here they had the greatest architect of all time: the man who designed the original course, was there from the beginning, and had earned the respect of Bobby Jones. Yet their comments were limited to a few questions concerning the addition of rough and the possibility of converting the greens to the new, super–short–growing bentgrasses to get even higher green speeds.

Were they merely humoring MacKenzie? Had they invited him to Augusta for their own amusement? As the day progressed, I sensed the committee had little or no interest in acting on any of his suggestions. I suspected they were there merely to enhance the content of their gossip at power lunches and cocktail parties.

"*I* know that my former associate, Perry Maxwell, relocated this greensite," Mac said from the middle of the tenth fairway, the beginning of the most famous nine holes in all of golf. MacKenzie's original design had the tenth green tucked next to the famous fairway bunker, but it had since been moved back to stretch the hole out to 485 yards. "I understand that this version of the tenth provides a better challenge for the professionals, but this is lunacy for your members. Can any of you hit and hold this green in two shots, or even three?"

More silence from the committee.

"Well, I see you have no interest in answering," MacKenzie said dryly. "Let us continue."

MacKenzie shook his head upon approaching the new eleventh tee. "Oh, my...A lot of strategy here!" he observed sarcastically, referring to the change in the tee shot angle from its original position to the right of the tenth green. The current view was a straightaway shot through a chute of trees to an enormously wide fairway. In MacKenzie's original dogleg-right design, the slope of the fairway and a right-center fairway bunker allowed for several options off the tee, including the opportunity for courageous players to cut the corner of the hole, leaving a short pitch shot as a reward. The Doctor made no comment about the eleventh green, where an undersized pond had replaced the creek to protect the green.

Feeling the stagnant heat of "Amen Corner" where the wind rarely blew in the summer, the Doctor loosened his tie before moving to the twelfth tee for a look at the most famous par-3 in tournament golf. He stood staring at the well-chronicled hole which on hot summer days like today was covered by a tent with misters to keep the bentgrass cool.

"The average players have no chance here, do they?" the Doctor asked the Committee.

Surprise, surprise — more silence.

"You have shrunk the green down to the size of a bread plate," Mac accused, criticizing perhaps the most celebrated par-3 on the planet. "How do you expect a player to play anything but a hit-and-hope shot? And those bunkers! Do you use a razor blade to trim and edge them every day, or just weekly, Mr. Jensen?" MacKenzie inquired sarcastically, referring to Augusta's meticulous grooming of the sand traps. If the Doctor expected a response from the superintendent, he got none.

Mac dropped his sarcastic approach and continued in a more moderate tone. "An ideal hole, which I felt this once was," he said, gesturing at the twelfth green, "should provide a considerable variety of shots according to the varying positions of the tee, the situation of the flag, the direction and strength of the wind, et cetera. It should also, at times, give full advantage to the voluntary pull or slice, a shot that only a few champions are able to carry out with any great degree of accuracy under pressure."

Still no response from the attentive committee.

"You know gentlemen, I have watched your tournament, and I have studied the shots hit to this twelfth hole. You are to be complemented for keeping the turf firm and for not giving into the mindless demands for rough over the years. However, when a hole such as the twelfth becomes nearly impossible to hit, it is really a matter of mere survival for the leading players, instead of an interesting challenge. You must not take all the options away from the players who want to try for more than just a straight shot to the middle of the green. Why do you think they call it Amen Corner? You've got to bloody hit your shot and pray that the golf gods like you! That is not the essence of the game — at least as I know it."

The Committee continued to listen but gave no hint of their reactions to the Doctor. They were in a difficult position. Twenty million people around the world see their course each year. Any change would be noticed, discussed and analyzed by every sportscaster, duffer and armchair architect in the world. Mac had to know that, but apparently he didn't care. This was a chance to release some feelings that had been suppressed for a very long time, and he was clearly enjoying it.

Instead of bothering to drive down to the twelfth green and the thirteenth tee, the Doctor led the group to the thirteenth fairway. He stood in awe of the distinguished hole and commented about its striking natural beauty. Then he announced that he wanted to inspect the green.

As we parked our carts near the narrow creek fronting the green and approached the grass-covered bridge, MacKenzie stopped to remind them to keep the water levels low in the creek, so that, as he put it, "you can really tempt and taunt the front rank players into going for the green when they are undecided. When they know that their ball might be playable in that creek, they are even more likely to take their chances going for the green."

Then Mac saw what he was afraid he had noticed on television.

"What on God's green earth is this bloody canal you have dug behind the green?" he demanded, pointing to a deep swale added behind the green to catch water runoff from the neighboring hillside. "And I see you used the dirt from this canal to elevate the green and create this freakish upper tier. Well, it looks simply awful!"

Jensen tried to defend the club's current version of the thirteenth. "Besides keeping water runoff from flooding the green, it really strengthens the hole," he said. "It was becoming too easy, and there were too many birdies."

"Oh, please!" MacKenzie snapped. "Tell that to the competitors in the Masters. I'm sure they will explain to you that under the pressure of the championship all birdies here are well-earned. Especially when the greens are so bloody fast that they are almost impossible to putt."

MacKenzie calmed down before speaking again. "To make this hole more troublesome, you've added difficulties to the rear of the green, punishing the bold player who successfully negotiates the hazard. Then you added a shelf in the green, making it nearly impossible to hit and hold within a reasonable range of the pin. Why not just erect a brick wall to prevent anyone from hitting their ball on in two shots?"

The changes to thirteen that MacKenzie raged about were always a source of conversation among Masters contestants. They were made under the supposed supervision of a former champion and were rarely criticized publicly because of the awesome nature of the thirteenth, which, despite what MacKenzie viewed as butchery, is still a phenomenal hole.

Standing in front of Augusta's fifteenth green, Mac spoke up again. "Why do you treat the bank of this lake like a bowling alley lane?" MacKenzie asked Jensen, drawing him away from the committee. He was referring to Augusta's practice of tightly mowing and rolling the lake bank for the Masters, forcing balls hit short of the green into the fronting water hazard. The practice had gotten so ridiculous that balls could actually find the putting surface, and then roll back without even having backspin.

"It's what I'm told to do," Jensen explained woodenly, fearful that an overheard comment might cost him his job. "We don't want a player who hits a bad shot to get lucky."

"Well, now," said MacKenzie, "I know that this hole has become too short for the modern professional, but don't you think these practices are a bit extreme? This bank rolls faster than most putting greens! Besides, it's a mistake to work so hard to eliminate the element of luck. You can no more eliminate the element of luck in golf than you can in everyday life. It is part of the game."

"What do you suggest we do with a par-5 that half the field reaches in two shots with a short iron?" Jensen asked somewhat bitterly.

"There is nothing you can do," MacKenzie replied. "The governing bodies of golf are the ones who need to step up and address the issue of equipment and the ball. If you had read my book, you'd know I warned of this problem in 1933, and things have only gotten worse since."

"How should they fix the problem?" Jensen asked.

"I always have been a strong believer in limiting the flight of the ball, and having seen how it has evolved since my day, I'm more convinced than ever it needs regulating," the Doctor said.

"Pleasure in achieving length is relative," he continued. "One of the problems with this solution is that any marked limitation of the flight of the ball is certain to be unpopular for some time after its inauguration. Golfers, especially those making a living playing the game, would dislike finding that they were unable to carry a bunker they were formerly able to carry. They would feel as though they had suddenly grown old. But that would change in due time, especially if the member tees were moved up a few yards. However, I see the drastic distance difference being with the professionals, not the average club player. Another benefit of a shorter ball is the return of the ground game. When the players have to use longer clubs to reach the green, they will resort to using the ground to help get them there, as we did in the old days."

"But what is so bad about courses having been lengthened to accommodate the current ball?" asked Jensen.

"Good God, man! Pace of play!" MacKenzie returned, almost shouting. "Something should have been done years ago. Golf courses have become far too long for most average players. Twenty years ago we played three rounds of golf a day and considered that we had taken an interminably long time if it took more than two hours to play a round. Today it is not unusual to spend over five hours!"

"But won't the equipment companies sue the governing bodies if they take any action?" Jensen asked.

"Let 'em bloody sue!" MacKenzie said, not really considering all of the dilemmas of regulating equipment. "Lord knows the governing bodies have the money to fight them — don't you read *Golf Digest*? Their job is to protect the integrity of the game, and I think it is safe to say they will not be doing that if they ignore the issue any longer!"

"But the governing bodies say the ball doesn't actually go any farther than it used to," Jensen continued. "They claim ball technology has just about reached its limit."

"That is utter rubbish!" MacKenzie retorted. "In my day, it was often suggested that we had already got to the limit of the flight of the ball. But every year it got two or three yards longer, and that adds up considerably over time. Of course, I did not believe a limit had been reached, as there is no limit to science, and I was correct. During the war, experts told us we had reached the limit of flight of a cannonball; then the Germans invented a gun that propelled a shell three times as far as it had ever been sent."

The committee members were now out of their carts and standing with me near the new sixteenth tee plaque honoring Arnold Palmer. Their attention had perked up with the talk about the ball. I suspected that a couple of the members might be USGA Committeemen.

"I don't understand what would be gained by regulating the ball, other than making a hole such as this one play a little longer for Tiger Woods and the other pros," Jensen said.

MacKenzie paused for a moment, marshalling his thoughts. "The professionals, as well as the amateurs, are losing the joy of playing the variety of approach shots that were necessary in the old days. Extreme length off the tee eliminates the challenge of certain holes, and quite often strips mid-length holes of their strategy. It's analogous to the lack of reading by youth today. By relying on motion pictures and television for their entertainment, they are missing the joys of reading and visualizing stories and exercising their imaginations."

*A*fter condemning the current sixteenth at Augusta as "the most out-of-place green he had ever seen on a golf course," the Good Doctor suggested they add some playable pin placements to the hole, because from what he could see there was only one interesting location: the Sunday final round position. I'm sure his hostility toward the hole had something to do with the fact that his original sixteenth hole had been abandoned in favor of the current version, a design collaboration between Bobby Jones and Robert Trent Jones. It didn't help that Mac had little regard for Trent Jones whom he had met in the early 1930s.

Mac was startled by the growth of the "Eisenhower Tree" off the seventeenth tee and he criticized the two fairway bunkers on number eighteen as being "completely out of character with the intentions of the original design and clearly the work of an amateur." He was right. The two bunkers, now a reasonable carry for Tiger and the longer hitters, were added in the 1960s to address Jack Nicklaus' prodigious length by MacKenzie's least favorite client, Clifford Roberts.

"*Y*ou really charmed them," I joked to Mac as the caravan arrived back at the clubhouse. I was amazed to see that most of the members actually thanked the Doctor for his time before heading into the air-conditioned clubhouse, though they made no attempt to ask questions or show any real interest in the good Doctor. How strange.

"They couldn't care less about what I had to say," MacKenzie sighed.

"Once you insulted their course, they shut down and didn't hear a word you said," I observed.

"How can *I* insult their course? I was the architect of this course, and I'm merely sharing constructive thoughts on how it has changed. That is an insult?"

"In today's society, Mac, you have to be more subtle with committees, and massage their egos a bit. I don't know if insulting is the word, but you definitely lost them early on with your criticism."

"How pathetic," Mac said. "That is completely irrational, Johnny, that's what it is. Get me a drink. I'm tired and thirsty."

*B*ob Jensen politely thanked us for coming and told Mac to send him a bill for a one-day site visit. He drove us to the airport, where the comfort of the private jet helped to finish what had been an unbelievably long day.

During a four-hour plane flight, I had time to reflect on the events of the day. Alister MacKenzie had returned to Augusta, and no one had documented his visit. Few questions were asked about his original design intentions, and frankly, the whole thing was weird. I realized that Mac was probably hurt by the lack of respect shown for his work there and that no one even took notes or photographs of the visit. I reminded myself to tell Mac when he awoke that I would like to type up a summary of his visit for posterity.

Then it finally dawned on me. The Augusta committee just wanted MacKenzie there for their own entertainment. This was not a courtesy visit, but rather, a curiosity visit.

10

$\mathcal{M}$ac and I returned to the Valley Club at 1:30 a.m. the following day to find forty-three messages on the voice mail line we had set up. Too tired to listen and sort out potential job candidates, I showed Mac how the system worked and drove back to the clubhouse cabins for some sleep. The Doctor had slept during most of the flight home from Augusta. I had tried to sleep, but I was busy to distracted by our luxurious private jet experience.

At home later, Mac woke me up with a phone call.

"I think I found a winner, Johnny," he said with genuine excitement in his voice. "It's everything I have been looking for. It's in San Diego, which I understand is only a few hours down the road."

"Huh?" I groaned, half asleep.

"Get dressed and bring our belongings, including some drawing materials. We are driving down this afternoon for a dinner meeting and, if we still have sunlight, a quick review of the site."

"What time is it, anyway?" I asked.

"Almost 10 a.m. Plenty of time to make it there before sunset. Meet me at the maintenance yard in fifteen minutes." He hung up.

I took a shower and made the short drive from the clubhouse cabins to the superintendent's office down the road. Before I left the cabins, I collected my laptop, our still–packed suitcases and my drawing tools.

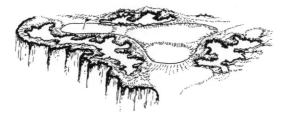

"*It's* called Pendleton Beach Golf Links," MacKenzie said as we drove down scenic Highway 101 through Ventura. "Have you heard of the project? It sounds promising."

I was so tired that I couldn't conceal my disgust. "Oh come on, Doc, you've got to be kidding. That project has been talked about since the early '80s. It's never going to be built."

"Evidently they have gotten all of their approvals and settled all of the lawsuits," Mac said. "The Coastal Commission, the Pentagon, and Lord knows who else have had a say in the matter. They also claim to have their finances in order, so they are ready to design and build the course."

"So where do we come in?" I asked, still not enthusiastic.

"They commissioned Billy Bell, Jr. to do a routing some time ago, but he passed away," said Mac. "They had not seriously pursued another architect because they assumed the project would never happen. But the man in charge heard we were available and asked if we could come down as soon as possible."

*P*endleton Beach Golf Links had first been proposed in 1983 by a group of retired, golf-addicted Camp Pendleton Marines. The property they chose for their dream course was just one small section of the base's vast holdings along the Pacific Ocean, about forty minutes north of downtown San Diego. Consisting of grassed-over dunes, sandy soil and undulating land, the "links-like" property had served for many years as the site of military exercises, particularly during the Gulf War when the terrain of Iraq had to be replicated.

As a bonus, the secluded golf course site was not visible from the well-traveled I-5 freeway. However, this semiprivate golf club did have one serious drawback: the San Onofre nuclear power plant lay just five miles away. Ten years later, the presence of the power plant proved to be quite handy when the group went before the Coastal Commission for preliminary approval: only one environmental group opposed the project, and they had no objection except to the use of chemicals on the course. The Marines assured the Commission that nonorganic fertilizers, pesticides and herbicides would rarely be used and even agreed to put various limitations in writing.

Even though they knew it would take years to get it approved, the group commissioned golf architect William F. "Billy" Bell in 1983 to route and design a full-length course. Bell, who designed California seaside courses at Torrey Pines and Sandpiper, died suddenly of a heart attack in 1984. But the group of retired Marines persisted in their efforts. In 1994, they finally got their big break when the government began closing and downsizing military bases.

Though the Camp Pendleton base would remain intact, the Pentagon offered up the golf course parcel for one dollar in return for access to the course for all United States veterans and their guests. I had not heard much about the project in recent months, other than that it was due to come up for approval before the California Coastal Commission again soon. Evidently they had finally won approval from the Coastal Commission, and the search was on for an architect.

When they heard Alister MacKenzie was available, the Marines wasted no time in calling. MacKenzie spoke to the group's lead investor, Colonel Joe Murdoch, and assured him that if the terrain was as good as he described, dirt moving would be required for tees, greens, and bunkers only. That meant the remainder of the budget could be spent on an irrigation system and a modest maintenance building.

Colonel Murdoch was enthusiastic to hear about MacKenzie's low-profile, inexpensive approach and asked him to come down as soon as possible. Why we couldn't wait another day I don't know, but within hours of their conversation, we were on the road to San Diego. Somehow, Mac was finding the energy to handle the jet lag, but I was exhausted. The three-hour drive south seemed to take twice that long.

"*C*an we talk about your demeanor a bit?" I asked as we drove through a typically overdeveloped section of Orange County en route to North San Diego.

"What about it, Johnny?"

"You cannot talk to these people like you talked to the committee at Augusta. These are clients. We might be working for them."

"It won't be a problem, Johnny! What're you worried about?"

"I'm concerned that you will tell them they are a bunch of Marines who don't know golf architecture from a hole in the ground and to mind their own business. That's what you will tell them!"

"Actually, I already did," MacKenzie said with a big grin, his bushy eyebrows rocketing up his bald forehead.

"WHAT?"

"When Colonel Murdoch asked if I was interested, I told him we would have to be left alone to design the course. He agreed and told me that all they want is a pleasurable course that veterans can play and enjoy. They aren't concerned about difficulty since the wind and grasses will cause enough trouble for the golfers anyway."

"What else did he request?" I asked suspiciously.

"That was it," Mac said. "I told him I thought we'd do it for a $100,000 design fee, and a $1.5 million construction budget. However, I told him you would give him firm numbers since I'm not up on the actual cost of things these days. We just need enough for a simple irrigation system, building materials and manpower. The colonel will be greeting us personally to go over the specifics."

"That's it?" I asked, thinking this all sounded too good to be true.

"That was it. Don't worry, I have everything under control," MacKenzie grinned.

"That's what I'm worried about," I said.

"Would you stop worrying? Colonel Murdoch is from the old school. He understands his place and even knows something about camouflage. I'm sure he will leave us alone. It will be fine. Trust me."

Oddly, I did.

11

Mac and I pulled up to the designated meeting spot at three o'clock. Colonel Murdoch greeted us in the parking lot of a dingy coffee shop near the Camp Pendleton base. A soupy fog lurked over the coastline, waiting to blanket the base and the surrounding area as it does nearly every afternoon. As he got out of the car, Mac's Scottish blood seemed to perk up at the scent of damp, salty air.

Joe Murdoch was a tall, impressive man, about 6-foot-1 with broad shoulders and a Marine crewcut that revealed a receding hairline. His strong handshake let me know that he had managed to remain fit since retiring over twelve years ago. After a few minutes of conversation over a cup of coffee inside the small restaurant, I knew why the Doctor had been so eager to see the proposed Pendleton Beach Golf Links.

The colonel was a dream client. He spoke modestly about the history of the project and his group's desire to create an enjoyable course that anyone could play, whether they were beginners from the base or retired veterans. The colonel also understood that he had something special with the linksland and the rural setting by the Pacific, secluded enough that players would not hear much noise from the military training areas or the freeway. Murdoch said that after Mac analyzed the site, he thought the commission would go to MacKenzie and Grant, and construction could start as soon as possible.

"You *think?*" Mac asked.

"Well, yes, uh, there is one stumbling block," Colonel Murdoch admitted.

At this point I wanted to tap Mac on the shoulder and say, "See, I told you so," but I restrained myself.

"What's the stumbling block?" the good Doctor demanded.

Murdoch gathered himself. "Well, you see, I am in charge of the project here, but I report to a committee, and..." he paused, searching for the right way to put it.

"And what?" Mac pursued.

"And they want to interview another architect as well, and perhaps meet you both simultaneously at the site and hear both of you present your thoughts on the project." Murdoch's normally square shoulders slumped a little, and he dropped his gaze and bent to take a sip of coffee.

Doctor MacKenzie shook his head. "I do not share my thoughts with other architects," he said. "And I surely did not come here to compete with anybody else. Nor did I come here to talk to a committee. I'm too old and too talented to engage in a petty competition that will only satisfy a committee that is trying to get some free advice."

Mac then looked at me. "Come on, Johnny, let's go."

Now, I had no right to speak up at this point, but I couldn't resist. Mac rose from our table and headed for the parking lot. I pretended to follow him, but looked over my shoulder and asked Colonel Murdoch a question.

"Who is the other architect?"

"It's Bill Mario." Murdoch said.

Mac stopped. I was too stunned to even think of the implications, but clearly the Doctor had a quick change of heart. He looked at me, returned to Murdoch and cocked his head.

"Let us have a look at the site," he said, "and then we'll decide whether we'll enter your little competition."

Murdoch gave Mac a look of pure gratitude. "Thank you," he said. "You are my only hope, you know. If you don't take the job, this beautiful site will be ruined."

"Before we get too far ahead of ourselves, why don't we have a look at what we're talking about?" said Mac.

"Of course, of course," Murdoch said, grabbing his jacket and paying the bill.

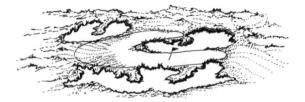

With two hours of sunlight left, we piled into the Explorer and got back on the freeway for the short drive to the property. We exited at Las Pulgas Canyon Road and took a narrow asphalt street toward the beach until we reached a gated chain-link fence. A small sign read, "Restricted Area, Personnel of the United States Military, ONLY." The colonel unlocked the small gate and we pulled onto a firmly packed dirt path.

"Colonel, don't ever taint this entrance with some big, ugly sign," the Doctor advised. "Leave that fence and 'Restricted Area' sign just as they are — it will add mystique to the place."

The colonel smiled and nodded in agreement.

I could hardly believe what I was seeing as we entered the property. Mac, on the other hand, had become accustomed to looking at remarkable sites during his career, so for him this was all in a day's work.

The property looked fairly level at first glance, but on closer inspection I noticed several dunes rising from ten to thirty feet high. We first drove by a sunken valley that could easily accommodate golf holes running in both directions. I knew right away that it would be the perfect place to run a few holes back and forth. We could even perch some tees on the sides of the subtle rises in the valley floor.

The entire property was covered with a light brown native grass that looked similar to fescue and bore a striking resemblance to Muirfield in Scotland. Clumps of what looked like Scottish heather sprouted here and there, adding to the authentic links feel. I knew that both heather and gorse, plants native to Scotland, were occasionally found in the damper climates of San Diego, though I thought it was pretty uncommon.

After a straight five-hundred-yard stretch, the dirt road drifted left and up a gentle slope, turning into asphalt at that point. Colonel Murdoch announced that we were nearing the clubhouse.

"So it's already built?" I asked.

"Yes, in a sense," the colonel replied. "Actually it is a converted lookout building that was built during the Second World War. We remodeled it, keeping the miniature lighthouse intact. We even left the old telescope. We put in a paved parking lot and built six bungalows, all of which have plumbing, electricity, and cable television. The entrance road has been paved only on this last portion since we weren't exactly sure where the golf holes would go."

I parked the car in the modest-sized lot and noticed the six little cabins built near the green-trimmed, white clubhouse. It was a nifty building, with just enough space for a comfortable grill room and a pro shop. The clubhouse was situated on a subtle rise that allowed a glimpse of the Pacific Ocean.

"We plan to build more bungalows when the course is open for play," the colonel said.

"You have what appears to be a fine piece of land," MacKenzie observed stiffly. He sounded a little reluctant to admit it. I interpreted that as, "I like it, but I'm really pissed off that I have to compete for this bloody job."

My attention to this point had been focused on the gentle linksland, but Mac's tone triggered an alert in my brain, and I held my breath, fearful that the good Doctor was about to say something intemperate.

Instead, he asked quietly, "May we walk the land for a while? I'm ready to consider a routing for the course." I was relieved. I knew that we were looking at the best available golf course property in the world, and I didn't care what we had to do to get the job. Even if it meant confronting my former boss.

The late afternoon fog finally moved in and covered the Pendleton Beach property. A cool breeze had kicked up, forcing me to put on my windbreaker. Doctor MacKenzie, Colonel Murdoch and I examined the original routing map which the colonel had retrieved from his office in the clubhouse. We walked slowly to Billy Bell's proposed site for the first and tenth tees.

"Umph!" MacKenzie muttered.

"I beg your pardon?" the colonel asked.

MacKenzie politely ignored the colonel and turned to me. "John, why is it that Americans have become obsessed with having set and predictable standards for everything they do? In golf courses, you always see the ninth hole return to the clubhouse. It has ruined so many potentially fine designs."

I pointed out the obvious. "It allows a golfer to start the course on either the front or back nine," I said. "And it's convenient for those who only have time to play nine holes."

"Yes, yes, I know that. Thank you," MacKenzie huffed before turning to address the colonel. "I was the first to write articles emphasizing the importance of the two loops of nine holes. During recent years in the United States, I have had more sleepless nights owing to committees being obsessed by this principle than anything else, and I have often regretted that I propounded it."

I was confused. Mac said he advocated two loops of nine, and then he said it was ruining golf.

The Doctor continued. "There are several fine aspects to this routing, Colonel. Don't misunderstand me. But is it true that your course is only going to have between fifty and a hundred players per day and will be closed on Monday mornings for maintenance?"

"That is my hope."

"Well then, as I see it, you really do *not* need the nines to return. If we were to do this project, we would build something that would take only three hours to play. And without the ninth returning to the clubhouse, the golfer will find that there is great charm in exploring fresh country and never seeing the same view twice until he arrives back at the clubhouse. It has worked for Cypress Point, Pebble Beach, Pine Valley, The National and many others."

The colonel laughed. "I hope we play that fast here and can be compared to those courses!"

Mac ignored the colonel's remark and pressed on. "Looking at this map," he said, "and with just a glance across the property, I already disagree with the location of some of the holes as they are marked here."

"I'm glad to hear that, because Mr. Mario thinks it is superb," the colonel said. "If you were to accept this commission, we would ask that you have the first hole start somewhere near the clubhouse and the final hole finish in front of the building so golfers can watch the others finish their rounds and enjoy the sunset."

I held my breath, fearing an outburst from Mac, whose old age had to be catching up to him after so many hours of traveling.

"That is acceptable and certainly understandable," MacKenzie pronounced to my relief. "I want you to know, and perhaps you can relay to your partners, that to make a course interesting for all classes of players, and at the same time offer a superior test of golf, the routing of the course is of paramount importance. A badly routed and planned course can be improved, but it can rarely be made perfect. It is like a badly-fitting coat. And understand, this is nothing against the work of Mr. Bell; I just have a different way of doing things."

The colonel nodded and MacKenzie continued.

"Every natural feature and contour should be carefully studied, and the design of the course should harmonize with these natural features. The natural contours of the ground should be used to create a series of swales, not only to create more interesting playing possibilities, but also to take care of drainage — though I understand you don't get much rain here in San Diego."

"No, we don't," the colonel agreed. "We are restricted by the Coastal Commission to only using small amounts of certain organic fertilizers and we don't plan to irrigate the course very often — an approach I know you support."

I liked the way this conversation was going. Mac seemed to be warming up to the project. I knew his change of heart was complete when he later launched into a lecture about approaches that I had heard earlier in the week.

"Absolutely," Mac agreed. "With the advent of irrigation systems and the senseless desire for green grass, nearly everyone today plays a coarse and vulgar pitch shot, which only punches a hole in the green and makes for dull golf. With the exception of the

Old Course at St. Andrews and few similar courses, there is rarely any necessity to play any other kind of shot. Golfers are losing the joy of playing the variety of approach shots that were necessary in the old days. So many once-fine layouts have become wet mud heaps disguised as golf courses, saturated in that eternal quest for green."

The colonel nodded again in perfect accord.

"The treatment for the approaches is almost as important as that for the greens," MacKenzie continued. "One of the most fascinating, if not *the* most fascinating of shots is the run-up approach we so frequently get on old seaside courses like St. Andrews. An approach of this kind cannot be made successfully if there is a defined margin between the approach and the green, or if the approaches and greens are kept soggy with water so that no other shot is possible except an inartistic pitch."

The colonel interrupted, "It has been difficult, but I think we have convinced the members that keeping the course green is too expensive and not the way the best golf is played."

MacKenzie grinned, exposing his brown, gapped teeth. "I had an old friend and associate, John McLaren, who was perhaps the greatest authority on public parks in America. He frequently expressed his fondness for green grass. I had to persuade him that the best golfing grasses vary in color. They may be red, brown, blue, dark green, light green, yellow, and at times even white or gray. A golf course that consists of only one shade of green is ugly. I cringe at the thought of the expense and work that goes into creating such an artificial appearance."

Then MacKenzie looked at Colonel Murdoch, sizing him up. This made me nervous again. I hate it when he sizes people up!

"Now, Colonel, this might seem like a strange request," Mac warned, "but I want you to consider turning rabbits loose over the property once we get the turf seeded."

"Rabbits?" Murdoch gave himself away, showing unusual surprise for such a well-trained military man. I wondered if this was my first hint that senility had kicked in for Mac. I remembered reading about rabbits in his books, and though it might have been practical in his day, imagine if he brought this up in front of Bill Mario! I made a mental note to tell him not to make an issue of the rabbits when we met with the committee.

"In the old days, one greenkeeper took care of the golf course and rabbits acted as the 'grounds staff,' keeping the turf short, crisp, and free from weeds," the Doctor explained. "Now, the rabbits have been killed off, and alkaline fertilizers — fit only for agriculture — are used. The result? The sparse, velvety turf has disappeared and has been replaced by plantains, daisies, clover and luscious agricultural grasses, which need an enormous amount of mowing, weeding and upkeep."

"Well, it's something we can consider," Murdoch said, not knowing what else to say. The more I thought about it, though, the more I actually liked the idea. Maybe the old guy was on to something.

"Good! You won't regret it," MacKenzie replied. "Now, I'm getting a bit tired. What do you say we go have something to drink and discuss this joint meeting with Mr. Mario. When is it, by the way?"

"Uh, first, uh, first thing tomorrow morning," Murdoch replied reluctantly. To my surprise, Mac just laughed.

After a few backward glances at the property, we drove to the local pub and ate dinner. We discussed the timeline for the

project, and MacKenzie said he was prepared to begin right away —
that is, if the committee selected us. He announced that it would
take a few days for us to settle on a routing we liked and to hire
some shapers. I had someone in mind, so I bounced it off Mac.

"I've heard of some excellent men, but I don't know if they are
available," I ventured.

"Oh really?" Mac said, trying to give me some credit in front
of Colonel Murdoch. "They have done good work?"

"Yes," I replied. "They have restored some of your bunkers and
I hear they have a great feel for your style."

"Give them a call, Johnny," Mac said, reminding me that I
had no idea how to get hold of them. It would be a long night on
the phone trying to track them down.

"I have a good sense for finding qualified men," Mac said,
addressing Colonel Murdoch. "This reminds me of a story that I
think about from time to time when I want to remember what
kind of man *not* to hire."

The colonel appeared interested, so Mac continued.

"In Britain at every big railway station, a man is employed to
walk the trains and tap the wheels with a hammer to find out from
the sound if the wheels are cracked. A bishop got into a conversation with one of these men and elicited from him that he had
worked for the railway company for thirty-five years and had never
had a day off.

"'Splendid!' the bishop said. 'What a good and faithful ser-
vant you are. If the country had more men like you what a magnificent country it would be to live in. Now tell me, why do you
tap on these wheels?' The faithful employee scratched his head
and said, 'Blowed if I know!'"

The colonel made the Pendleton Beach cabins available to us and said that if we got the job, any workers who needed to stay there were welcome.

"Johnny, let's head on back and get some rest. We have a long day ahead of us tomorrow."

Murdoch seemed to be relieved that dinner at the pub had gone well and that Mac was still interested in the job. "Thanks so much for giving us a chance," Murdoch said. "I know it is ridiculous that you have to compete against Bill Mario, but he is one of the biggest architects in the business, and the committee wants to hear what he has to say."

I laughed, and Murdoch gave me a quizzical look.

"It's nothing, Colonel," I said.

"Just ignore him," Mac said. "What time are we expected to be prepared tomorrow?"

"Be at the clubhouse at 9:00 a.m.," Murdoch said.

Mac's big smile indicated that he welcomed the challenge lying ahead. "We'll be there."

12

"*I* don't see this course having just *one* signature hole," Bill Mario was telling four Pendleton Beach committeemen as Mac and I approached the proposed first tee area. "I see you having *eighteen* signature holes here at Camp Pendleton Beach Country Club."

This was a classic line from the Mario repertoire, though he normally gets the name of the course right.

"The main deficiency I see here, and don't take this the wrong way, but the land just doesn't have enough movement to satisfy the tastes of modern golfers and course–ranking panelists," Bill continued, oblivious to Mac and me, who had walked up from behind and were now just a few feet away.

Bill was so full of himself that he didn't even notice that the whole committee was staring at Mac and me as we approached from the clubhouse. He was more concerned with using expressive hand gestures for his official photographer who had made the trip down to get a few shots of Bill in action.

"You'll probably need to move about 750,000 cubic yards," Bill said, at the same time computing his percentage from the construction company, in which he owned a small stake. My guess was that he received ten cents for every cubic yard he ordered moved and a lot more for every change order he made to the original construction plans. But I could never verify it while I was working for him.

"Pushing that much dirt will give the ground lots of move-ment and really create a links style course," Bill concluded, smil-ing, probably thinking he had the job all locked up. But Colonel Murdoch had heard enough. He was among the four committee-men, who presumably had been listening to Bill blow smoke for the last few minutes.

"Mr. Mario, this is Doctor Alister MacKenzie and his partner, John Grant," Murdoch said, pointing us out. Bill whirled around. Our eyes met and I could see he was shocked. I don't know what startled him more — seeing me or the good Doctor. Since Bill was stunned into speechlessness, Mac made the first move by greet-ing him with a cool, civil handshake. I did the same but I added a little grin and a confident grip that I hoped would give Bill pause.

"So this is who you landed with, John?" Bill gulped, trying to recover his equilibrium. "This is great, I thought you…"

"Well, we'd better start walking the terrain to compare ideas," Mac interrupted, saving me from an awkward moment in front of the committee.

"Yes, yes," Colonel Murdoch agreed hurriedly.

𝒯his had to be the strangest scenario I had ever seen in the golf architecture business. Two architects interviewing at the same time and each the antithesis of the other. There was the old Scot who believed in working with the land, and strategically placing bunkers so that the golfer had to think his way around the course.

Then there was Bill, who built pretty pieces of landscape architecture at inflated prices.

Naturally, I was apprehensive about such an awkward scenario, but at least Mac was there for support. And Mac seemed to understand how awkward the situation was. He told me earlier in the morning to stay positive and keep my mouth shut. Which I did. Well, for a while anyway.

"Mr. Mario has been telling us what he thinks of our property and how we should proceed on our project," Colonel Murdoch said, addressing Mac and me after we had been introduced to the rest of the committee.

"Can you tell us your thoughts, Doctor MacKenzie?" Murdoch asked, while the group of retired military men listened intently.

"Well, to begin with, thank you for inviting us here to your lovely property," Mac said, in a glowingly gracious voice he had warned me to expect. Mac said this was the first, last and only time I would see him in his "salesman mode."

"You have one of the finest properties for golf that I've ever been privileged to see," he continued, unabashedly laying on the flattery. "It has all of the essentials for good golf: rolling terrain, wind, sandy soil, and the Pacific Ocean potentially in play on a few holes. Very little dirt will need to be moved, perhaps only enough to shape the greens, tees and to camouflage some bunkers. Otherwise, it is nearly perfect terrain for golf."

Colonel Murdoch interrupted. "Mr. Mario feels that many thousands of cubic yards of dirt must be moved to make it particularly spectacular. What do you think?"

The Good Doctor looked at the faces of all the committee-men, then at Mario. Either he was going to give a distinguished and diplomatic reply, or the cranky old Scot was finally going to show his true colors.

"Well, that would be one way to approach the project," Mac said reasonably. I couldn't believe it. Since when did he become so politically correct? And since when did he ever endorse taking perfect linksland and moving dirt all over the place? He couldn't be serious.

"It would certainly give you some splendid views of the Pacific and more mounding would bring a touch of Ireland to the course...a Ballybunion look," Mac continued.

Bill was nodding, looking pleased that MacKenzie apparently understood his convoluted method for ruining a wonderful piece of natural land. Something was seriously wrong here, but I followed Mac's advice and kept my mouth shut. I think even Colonel Murdoch was stunned by Mac's uncharacteristic response, but I could tell he was relieved that at least none of the committee had been individually insulted. Murdoch posed another question.

"Mr. Mario says that the original routing is wonderful, but that he has to add an irrigation lake somewhere on the course to supply water, rather than relying on our well and having to pay for water from the District. Do you agree?"

Even MacKenzie struggled with this one, looking questioningly at Mario for an explanation. There was something about Mac — a presence, an aura — that intimidated everyone around him — including Bill Mario.

"Yes, that is right," Bill confirmed. It dawned on me that Bill did not have his usual fawning entourage along for the trip, except for his photographer. I guessed this must have been at Colonel

Murdoch's request. I knew that without his "prompters," Bill was in trouble.

"Since you have such an arid climate here," Bill continued, "I recommend a large lake down in the valley you see when you first drive in. A lake would not only create a stunning aesthetic feature, but it would also provide water to keep things lush and green during the summer when you don't get any rain and the water bills can get pretty high. The lake could also feed some sort of waterfall landscaped entrance, should you decide to build such a thing."

No one responded, though I was getting ready too. The silence was making Bill nervous, so he kept talking to fill the void. When I worked for him, these moments of silence were my cue to break in and save his rear end before he said anything too stupid. This was going to be fun.

"I would bulkhead the lake and use railroad ties all over the property so you would really get the feeling of old Turnberry," Bill went on.

"Prestwick," I corrected automatically, failing on my promise to stay quiet.

"I beg your pardon?" Bill asked.

"Prestwick," I repeated. "That's where the railroad ties are. Pete Dye got the idea to use railroad 'sleepers' from Prestwick and other courses that are located near railroad lines."

"Oh, of course, I always get them confused," Bill said. Then he looked at the committee. "You know, Prestwick and Turnberry are right next door to each other."

This guy is such a moron. "No, they are not, Bill," I corrected him. "Troon, not Turnberry, is next to Prestwick."

Mac giggled. I think he was getting close to breaking, but I had already reached my limit. Since it was apparent he was not going to chime in, I kept going.

"And Bill, moving thousands of yards of dirt will not improve this property, it will only make it look out of character with the terrain. Golf began as a ground game with the subtle undulations providing the most charming and interesting shots. A bunch of stupid looking mounds and artificial lakes make it an aerial game, not to mention that they would ruin this property."

Oops. I had slipped. So much for diplomacy.

"Now, now, Johnny, let's not be rude," Mac interrupted, suddenly the authority on decorum. "Though you do have a point that mounding up this course might look out of place with this lovely, gently rolling terrain."

Bill was fuming. "I resent your tone, John. I believe in building quality courses with lots of movement because that is what the golfers want these days. They want visually stunning courses, not these boring old, easy courses like MacKenzie and the other so-called master architects built," Mario said defensively. "I mean, look at Augusta and all of the work they had to do to make it great. They've added mounds, lengthened it and got the bunkers looking cleaner and better than ever."

Score a double bogey there for Bill. Just when I thought I had said the dumbest thing I could, old Billy came through for me. Mount St. MacKenzie was about to erupt, and the committee seemed to be enjoying the whole thing.

"Well, say what you will about Augusta," Mac said, way too calmly for my taste buds, "but if you took the time to study my original work there, you would know that my design was quite excellent and has only been altered out of ignorance to accommodate a golfing country unable to regulate its equipment or accept that the best players will shoot low scores under benign conditions."

Why was Mac being so nice all of a sudden?

"Putting in a lake has to be the dumbest thing ever," I interrupted. "All that a lake will do is look horribly out of place, run up the bill for construction, and put pressure on the superintendent to keep the course green year round."

Bill just shook his head at me, trying to come up with a response. But I wasn't done with him just yet.

"Bill, Doctor MacKenzie has designed three courses that are consistently ranked among the top five in the world — Augusta, Cypress Point and Royal Melbourne," I stated, knowing that I was about to touch a very sensitive nerve in Bill Mario. "How many courses do you have ranked in the top 100 in the world?"

Mac interrupted before Bill could answer. "Johnny — now, now. You know that those rankings have no real meaning. They were created for commercial purposes only, and have little relevance to me. Though, Mr. Mario, how many courses *do* you have in the world ranking?"

I had to hand it to Mac. He could be subtle and yet so brutal if he wanted to be.

Bill, who had already made a couple of double bogies in a row, then made at least a triple.

"Well, I bet you charge more than you deserve and use those rankings to back your inflated fees," Bill said in a pathetic comeback. He didn't know that MacKenzie and Grant had already proposed that the project could be done for $1.5 million dollars, with a $100,000 design fee. And now he was about to reveal his own quotation.

"You should know, Mr. MacKenzie," Bill said, already forgetting that he was talking to the Good Doctor, "that I quoted the total price for Camp Pendleton Beach Country Club at under $7 million, and," he finished triumphantly, "I reduced my fee to my pre-Architect of the Year rate of $500,000."

The committee stared at Bill as if he'd just arrived from another planet. Mac grinned, as did Colonel Murdoch, and even I cooled to a simmer, knowing that Bill had just shot himself in the foot.

"Well," Colonel Murdoch interrupted, "why don't we go for a walk around the property."

From that point on, we toured the land with strained civility. For the most part I kept my mouth shut and Bill stayed pretty quiet, falling to the back of the group for most of the tour. From time to time, Bill had the temerity to question Doctor MacKenzie, but the committee wasn't interested in what Bill had to say.

Meanwhile, Doctor MacKenzie charmed the committeemen to death, telling old stories of his favorite clients, from Bobby Jones and Marion Hollins to Fielding Yost, the man who commissioned him to build the University of Michigan course.

"I believed in economy of construction," Mac said. "We built only 22 bunkers at Augusta because the terrain played such an important role in the design. Here, I could see more bunkers to add zest to the strategy. Built properly and taking advantage of the many small rises and slopes, the hazards could be as superlative as those we built at Cypress Point."

"Perhaps the bunkers will take on individual names, like at St. Andrews," Colonel Murdoch pointed out, with the committee not quite understanding his point. Murdoch addressed his friends. "You know, guys, the 'Beardies' bunkers, or the 'Hell' bunker, or 'The Principal's Nose.' Remember when it took me five shots to get out of 'Walkinshaw's Grave,' and you all wanted to rename it after me!"

The committee members nodded and laughed, now remembering what the colonel was referring to. Mac and I glanced at each other, realizing that the committee had visited the Old Course at St. Andrews at some point, which would make our job easier when it came time to sell them on some characteristic of the design that resembled the Old Course.

"Gentlemen, you've reminded me of a favorite story of mine," Mac said, turning up the Scottish accent several notches for dramatic effect. "An English lady was travelling by carriage from

Edinburgh to the North, to catch the old ferries that used to run over the Firth of Forth before they had bridges. After her journey across the Firth, she wrote to a friend describing the journey."

Mac then changed his voice to a falsetto, imitating the English woman writing her letter. "It was pleasant enough till I got to a station called Leuchars, where two strange looking men got into my carriage. Their clothes were shabby, their whole appearance was wild and unkempt, and, though they spoke English with little accent, it was mixed with many strange words which I did not understand. *Niblick* was one. *Cleek* and *stymie* were some others I remember."

The committeemen were smiling, anticipating the humor in Mac's story. The Doctor continued in his female voice: "And these strange men talked in a horrid way about clearing somebody's nose, and running over somebody's grave; but worst of all was when one told the other how he had been in Hell that morning, but his partner had taken him out with a long spoon! I was very glad when we got to the next station because they were clearly mad, and thankfully they went on board the steamer which crosses the Tay."

*B*y the time we reached the clubhouse it was abundantly clear who would get the Pendleton Beach commission. I had not done much to ingratiate myself with the committee. However, Mac's performance was enough to win them over. Bill left rather quickly without shaking many hands when Colonel Murdoch informed us that the committee would be meeting and notifying us of their decision in the next day or so.

"I'm sorry I sort of lost it out there," I told Mac when we got back to the cabins.

"What do you mean? You came in right on cue!"

"What?" I asked. "You said to keep my mouth shut and I didn't. But I just had to answer some of Bill's ridiculous ideas."

"Yes you did — quite eloquently, I might add!" MacKenzie said.

"How come you let Bill get away with some of those stupid comments?" I asked.

"Because if I lost my temper and set that man in his place, I would have forfeited my credibility and we would never have been hired," Mac said. "We can repair your credibility over time, but if mine was lost, we would not have received the commission."

"So you agreed with me when I nailed Bill on his ridiculous suggestions?" I asked.

"Oh, believe me, I was right there with you, but there was no way I could say what I felt."

"So you knew I would lose my temper?" I asked.

"I counted on it. I knew your youth would get the best of you when you saw your old boss. By the way, he proved to be even less intelligent than I imagined!"

That afternoon, Mac and I looked over the topographic maps and discussed the property. I finally tracked down the famed shapers, Dan and Dave, who were conveniently unemployed at the moment and thrilled at the prospect of working with Mac if we got the job.

Sure enough, Colonel Murdoch called late that same day to tell us the good news: we were hired, and they were ready for us to start building the Pendleton Beach Golf Links as soon as possible. The news was almost anticlimactic. But we celebrated with a toast of scotch and spent several hours having a laugh at Bill Mario's expense.

13

"This is how we're going to do it," Mac announced the following morning. We were sitting at the breakfast table in the rarely used Pendleton Beach clubhouse, drinking coffee and nibbling on an assortment of fresh fruit and danishes that had been delivered earlier that morning.

"First, let's walk the land and look at a routing I sketched out last night," MacKenzie said. "Don't be afraid to speak your mind if you don't like what you see. I'm not as sharp as I used to be, so I could miss something here or there...but it's unlikely."

I had to show off a little. "Like the time you and Perry Maxwell did the routing for Crystal Downs and had only eight holes on the front nine?"

Mac just grinned. "That one got passed down over the years, eh?"

"You betcha it did!" I replied.

"Well, it is true," Mac said. "They had to feed me a pretty steady diet of my favorite scotch, Black and White, just to get me up there because, as you know, it's in the middle of bloody nowhere. Perry and I did have fun laying out that first nine holes because it is a wonderful property. We were patting ourselves on the back for such a fine routing on the front and admiring the view from atop the hill on the eighth. Frankly, we were really savoring that first nine, or eight as it turned out. Then Perry decided to do his arithmetic, and sure enough we were short, but thankfully there was a chance to have a nice uphill par-3 with a large dropoff to the left, so no one noticed."

"*O*nce we walk the property, I'm going to give you rough sketches so you can create one of those pretty, straight-lined maps that you make," MacKenzie joked. "No, on second thought, it's time for you to learn how to draw. I want you to copy my style — no straight lines, and I want to see plenty of soft edges!"

"Okay," I replied, too tired to argue with his lecture. The strain, the jet lag and the lack of sleep were really catching up with me. Of course Mac seemed fresh as a daisy.

"Don't you ever sleep?" I had to ask.

"Not much," MacKenzie said. "You'll be old one day — you'll see. Now, once we settle on a final routing I'm going to begin thinking through the individual holes. We'll walk them and discuss the strategy and how it can be enhanced. I'll give you a rough idea of what I have in mind, and then if you feel it is necessary, you can make any additions, subtractions, or suggestions you wish. But don't waste my time with useless propositions just for the sake of proving to me what you know. I trust your opinion, Johnny, so don't feel that you *have* to say something."

"Fine, fine..." I said, too tired to even care what he was saying. Like I was going to argue with the creator of Cypress Point?

"By the time we get a few of these holes sketched out, those shapers will hopefully be here and they can start building bunkers and greens," MacKenzie said. "I will ask you to oversee most of the fieldwork and the installation of the irrigation system, since I will get nauseated seeing those irrigation lines installed."

"What about the USGA-recommended greens mix and gravel?" I asked. "And the drain tiles? Don't we need to place an order for all of those materials?"

"Johnny, didn't you look at that sandy base out there?" Mac scolded me. "My word, I thought you knew better. We aren't touching a thing here except for adding some irrigation lines and throwing down some grass seed. I've gotten more black marks over the years for my drainage work than anything else, so I suppose we could consult someone, but I think things will drain just fine."

"What about grasses?" I asked.

"I'm leaving the green seed up to you. But with that native grass mowed down and topped off with some fescue, some perennial rye seed, and maybe some bent, we ought to be just fine. Those have always worked for me in the past. As for the greens, I'm sure any of the modern grasses will do fine. This is the perfect growing climate for virtually any grass, so I'm not worried. For bunker sand, let's give the native soil a chance — the particles look pretty good. If it doesn't work, I suppose we can truck some in."

I had to inject some common sense here. "You know we could get sued by Colonel Murdoch and his investors if things don't grow and we didn't at least run some soil tests. And I am afraid to think what will happen if we don't build USGA-conforming greens."

"Ah those bloody things are a headache these people don't need." MacKenzie waved his hand dismissively. "No one has proven to me that they work in arid climates like this. Look at all of the courses I have built in similar climates. I haven't heard any complaints about the quality of turf at Pasatiempo, or Cypress Point, or Royal Melbourne."

*A*fter breakfast we strolled to the clubhouse patio area that would one day overlook the first and eighteenth fairways. It was a typical north San Diego summer day. Low morning clouds produced a glare-free gray sky, and the temperature was a comfortable 67 degrees. The salty smell of the Pacific was particularly noticeable during the peaceful morning hours.

"Golf is a game and not a mathematical business," the Doctor said as we stood on the porch looking out over the site. "In your routings — for that matter in any creative thing you do — it is of vital importance to avoid anything that tends to be simple and stereotyped. Every effort should be made to increase the variety, mystery, charm and elusiveness of whatever it is you are undertaking, whether it be a building, a painting, or a golf hole. That way the members never get bored with playing it."

"What are you trying to say?" I asked, my lack of experience starting to show.

"The point is that we're not going to have any preconceived notions about the route we're taking here. I've made a sketch of the property and the primary undulations, and I've made a preliminary plan that takes into consideration the wind, the sun and other variables. Today I am looking for green sites, and most of all, a variety of the best holes we can find, both difficult and interesting."

"What's par going to be for the course?" I asked.

"Good Lord, boy — aren't you listening?" MacKenzie exclaimed. Now that is exactly what I mean about preconceived standards! The total yardage and par are meaningless — look at the Eden at St. Andrews — it's only 5900 yards, but certainly it's a fine test of golf. I am looking for 18 pleasurable holes.

Haven't we talked enough about how your contemporaries have decreed the law as to the total length of the course and the stagnating effect it has had on the game? Your generation is obsessed with a formulaic mentality. Remember — variety, charm and character always take priority over whatever so-called 'norms' are expected of the course."

MacKenzie paused to let me absorb his comments, though I refused eye contact, instead looking ashamedly at the ground. I knew what he was saying, but I was still just a little overwhelmed by the notion of working with *the* Alister MacKenzie.

"It is true, however, that there are certain general considerations that should influence us in the routing," the Doctor continued. "It is an advantage to start off with a few long holes to get people away quickly. It is also advisable to arrange the short holes so they will serve as a respite after one or more of the long ones. We should be influenced primarily by the nature of the ground and what is going to give the best test of golf and the most lasting pleasure."

"What do think of short par-4's?" I asked, trying to earn back some credibility.

"Many of your and my contemporaries have vulgarly stated that holes of the short two-shot variety are a 'drive and spit,' which can only be designed by those with no imagination whatsoever. I disagree. Not only do these holes provide excitement and greater interest for all levels of play, they are some of the best holes I know in golf. Look at the seventh, twelfth and sixteenth at the Old Course, or the eighth and ninth at Cypress Point — they are wonderful holes! Nothing is sadder in the modern game of golf than the extinction of the short par-4."

"And what about par-5's?" I asked.

"On most courses the three-shot holes are extremely dull, but sometimes, like the fourteenth at St. Andrews or the thirteenth at Augusta National, they can be fascinating. I prefer those that play as long two-shotters for the very long hitters. Conversely, lengthy two-shot holes should be interesting three-shotters for weaker players. I have to say that I am proud of the impact the thirteenth at Augusta has had, and it is basically a par-4½. However, I've noticed lately that short three-shotters are viewed quite negatively as not providing enough of a test. Only those ignorant of the spirit of the game would view a par-5 in such a way."

"That is true," I agreed. "A lot of people today don't like to build short par-5's because good players can reach them in two shots and make relatively easy birdies."

"That's nonsense! You talk to any top-ranked player and he will tell you there is no such thing as an easy birdie. You have to play fine shots to make birdies, especially in tournament play. Pars can come all sorts of ways, but birdies mean someone played skillfully. You can tell the critics that those so-called easy three-shotters can become psychologically frustrating when the players don't make the expected birdie."

"Can we start walking now?" I pleaded, impatient to start designing my first course with the good Doctor.

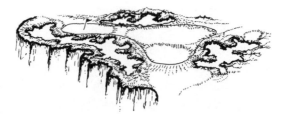

Mac carried a large sketchpad and a black pen, making notes on one page and slashing a few lines on another. I carried the topographic map and a pencil to note the green sites we selected.

As we walked the area for the proposed first hole, I noticed the unique nature of the native grass. From a distance it appeared thick and nasty, but on closer inspection it was sparse, meaning golf balls would be found fairly easily and played from it with just some hindrance from the tall grass.

After walking about 350 yards, Doctor MacKenzie declared that the green site he had penciled in for hole number one was at our feet and that the area just outside the patio would make a fine first tee.

"It has a nice, wide open landing area, but you have to play a straight or hooking tee shot to open up the best angle on the second shot to the green if you want a chance at birdie."

"Then the second hole can go down to the ocean," I anticipated.

"No! Number two is going back to the entrance road as a short three-shotter with a green perched just in front of the asphalt entrance street, similar to the Road Hole at St. Andrews. I spotted that one two days ago when we drove in."

"Why there?" I asked dubiously.

"I like teasing the golfers with the smell of the ocean before turning inland," MacKenzie explained. "It will make the finishing holes that much more rewarding. Besides, based on my interpretation of the property line, if we go to the cliff tops from here we'll be out of acreage to the north because of the property line."

"No, no," I said. "I meant, won't there be a problem if we put the green at the edge of the road? That's be a safety liability — we can't be within 150 feet of a road!"

MacKenzie laughed. "There will be about thirty or forty slow-moving cars coming and going here per day. I doubt that it will be an issue. Though with all the bloody lawyers running about, you never know."

*A*nd so it went the rest of the day, Mac and I walking the property and imagining a golf course into existence. I managed to convince the stubborn old man to modify his stance a few times, but most of the original ideas were his — and they *were* good.

We walked the tentative front nine in about two hours. The result was an oddly uniform nine, with two par-5's and two par-3's. A natural ridge of grass-covered dunes would run the length of the par-4 fourth and fifth holes and also help create a severe par-3 for the sixth — most likely an adaptation of the famous Redan hole at North Berwick.

The seventh would play to the flattest and least interesting part of the property. The Doctor remarked that the holes on this portion of the grounds would resemble the Old Course in strategy and feel because of their open, wind-exposed nature. Mac decided that an abandoned wooden fence to the left of the proposed seventh should come right to the edge of the green and be played as out-of-bounds. It would make for terrifying second and third shots. He measured the hole at approximately 565 yards.

Number eight would be a long dogleg-right par-4. Though the fairway was wide open, it required a well-placed drive to open up the view to a green that would be fronted by some attractive grass-covered dunes.

The ninth was penciled in as a short par-4 from an elevated tee and would play across two large ridges to a green that would be patterned after the final green at the Old Course of St. Andrews, complete with a "Valley of Sin." Mac noted that the ninth might be driveable for a good player if the prevailing wind wasn't blowing too hard, but the two ridges bisecting the fairway would create some fascinating stances for the short approach shot. As might be expected after MacKenzie's lecture on routings, the ninth hole did not return directly to the clubhouse, though it was within reasonable walking distance.

We mapped out the tenth, a long par-4 that would play into the breeze and give the back nine a stern beginning. The par-5 eleventh doglegged slightly around a ridge of native grasses and could be reachable by the better players because of a helping breeze. The greensite for the eleventh was particularly enticing; it would sit in a bowl below some dramatic heather-covered dunes.

There was another advantage to the eleventh green site: it finished close to the clubhouse, allowing us to stop for a much needed lunch break.

*A*fter consuming fresh turkey sandwiches that had been delivered while we were out surveying the property, Mac and I returned to routing the back nine. Of course the Doctor had a nip of scotch with his lunch to help him fight off the urge to take a nap.

So far, MacKenzie's preliminary drawing from the night before, which he had based on the topographic map, was nearly identical to what we decided on after the initial walking tour of the property. The only exceptions were a few green sites that we mutually agreed had to be moved to take advantage of various natural features.

The twelfth would be a quirky two-shotter, playing about 375 yards uphill into the prevailing breeze. The second shot would be semi-blind because of a tall ridge some 260 yards from the tee, though I mentioned to Mac that a few hours of 'dozer work could eliminate the problem.

A 1930s MacKenzie might have scoffed at such a suggestion, but the Doctor kindly explained that leaving the ridge in the fairway created a blind second shot unless the player hit a big drive and carried the ridge. Mac reminded me of how several holes at Royal St. George's were ruined because the club eliminated several blind shots. He felt that at least one blind shot on the course merely lent more variety, but I was still skeptical. Mac promised me that there would be some remarkable bunkers sculpted out of the back hillside to provide the golfers with something to aim at, making the blind nature of the second shot acceptable.

The thirteenth tee sat atop a nice dune not far from the shoreline. MacKenzie envisioned it playing downwind to a "punchbowl" green, but I preferred building a version of the eleventh, or High hole at St. Andrews. MacKenzie agreed to consider my suggestion or perhaps even let the shapers come up with something special on their own.

The course turned inland one last time with the short par-4 fourteenth, which we agreed was one of the more interesting green sites on the property. It would be sandwiched between the only exposed sand dunes on the property, with a long, angled green.

The home stretch included the fifteenth, a murderous par-4 that would play into a quartering wind from the right, thus making it a virtual three-shot hole for the average player. The sixteenth was a par-3 along the cliffs overlooking the ocean, and the seventeenth would be a par-4 with the ocean very much in play on the left, though Mac said he wasn't sure what else he would do with those holes.

MacKenzie wavered between building the eighteenth as a brutal downwind two-shotter, or as a shorter par-5 that many of the members could reach in two shots. I suggested that the green could finish right up against the club patio and play as a par-5, with out-of-bounds to the rear of the putting surface à la Royal Troon or the Old Course.

"Yes," Mac said. "With the patio and a nice stone wall to the rear of the green, it will be just like the home hole at St. Andrews. I used to love to listen to some of the old cronies who'd lean on the railings overlooking that green."

"That will be nice," I said, glad that Mac shared my vision. "The members can sit out on the patio, eat lunch and watch their friends play up to the finish," I said, basking in the glory of my great idea.

"Well, let's not get too carried away," Mac cautioned.

"Why not?"

"Because it reminds me of the time I was playing Portrush with a friend who happened to be a deaf old Scotsman. When we were close to reaching the fifth green out near the cliffs, I expressed my admiration of the scenery, the greens and things in general. I continued on and on about the lovely surroundings until we finally arrived at the green, which was guarded in the rear by cliffs covered by rooks."

"What's a rook?" I asked.

"It's an old sea crow," Mac said. "Anyway, I remarked to my playing partner, 'Isn't it delightful to hear the rooks?'

"To which the deaf old Scotsman said, 'Come again?'

"So I repeated a bit louder, 'Isn't it delightful to hear the rooks?'

"To which the old Scot replied, 'I can't hear a word you're sayin' for those damned crows!'"

14

When Mac and I walked off the proposed eighteenth green site, we were greeted by two men dressed in typical golf course shaper attire: dingy khakis, weathered boots and loud-colored golf shirts. They were also wearing new hats proudly displaying the last project they worked on.

"I'm Dan, and this is Dave," the taller, more outgoing of the two said with a smile, offering his hand.

"Thank you so much for coming," Mac replied, greeting the men with uncharacteristic warmth. "I've heard many good things about your work from John. I understand you have studied many of the classic courses and that you can shape just about anything to hoodwink us into believing the artificial was made by Nature."

"Well, I don't know...that's awful nice of you, sir," Dan said. Dave, the quiet one, still said nothing.

"Men, it's 'Mac' to you!" the Doctor said. "Now, meet John Grant, whom you have spoken to on the phone. He will be assisting you with the construction details and the interpretation of my drawings."

Dan and Dave greeted me with the usual shaper vs. design associate animosity, even though I was the one responsible for them being here. I don't know what it is, but in my years with Bill Mario, no matter how nice I was, shapers always hated the guys who came from the office.

Sensing the tension, MacKenzie offered Dan and Dave some reassurance.

"John understands what it will take to make this a fine course," he said. "I trust you will all get along well together, and he will provide you with whatever you need!"

Finally Dave, the quiet one, spoke. "We met Colonel Murdoch and he showed us our rooms. What time do you want us here tomorrow?" Dave was clearly focused on the job at hand and bored with small talk.

"Whenever you men would like," MacKenzie replied. "I will get some sketches together of the first few greens and you can have them tomorrow. We don't plan on moving much earth, so your work will consist mostly of clearing and removal of some of the unwanted heather, and shaping the bunkers and building some real MacKenzie greens."

Mac thought for a moment, then pointed toward the site of the future golf course.

"If you decide to get to work before I arrive tomorrow morning, this will be the first tee. The hole will move straight away with the fairway center about thirty-five yards to the right of that large dune on the left. You can rough out a nice-sized tee tomorrow morning," Mac said.

"What style of bunkers do you want us to build?" Dan asked.

"I'm glad you asked that, Dan," Mac said. "It is very easy. Old Patty Cole, my longtime bunker shaper and sod expert, had the best system, which always served us well. He'd just look up in the sky and pick a floating cloud and try to copy its shape and its irregular lines. The little white floaters after a rain make the best bunkers, but I'm sure you men know what I'm looking for."

Dan and Dave nodded.

I included myself in the discussion. "The colonel promised to have some equipment deliv—"

"It's already here," Dave interrupted. So much for my first stab at being one of the guys.

"Greeeaaat," MacKenzie purred, suddenly in a more mellow mood than any I had seen in our time together. I wondered if his spirits had been encouraged by a wee nip more of scotch when I hadn't been looking.

"Well, I don't know about you boys, but I have to get to work," the Doctor said, heading off toward his cabin.

"But don't you want to have some dinner?" I urged, not exactly thrilled at the prospect of being abandoned with two guys who apparently did not like me much.

"No, no, I have work to do. Besides, I have all I need," Mac said, turning with a huge grin on his face and, sure enough, drawing his trusty traveling bottle of scotch from an inside pocket.

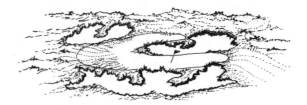

The cabins at Pendleton Beach provided everything you could want: large beds with firm mattresses, thin pillows that wouldn't throw your neck out of position, cable television with seventy channels to choose from, and an old-fashioned shower with an abundance of water pressure. After taking full advantage of the amenities, I went to bed, only to hear the phone ring right after I had fallen asleep.

"Hel...lo?" I answered groggily, looking at the alarm clock but seeing only a blur of digital red lights.

"Johnny, get up! I have two beauties ready to go."

"But it's 12:15 a.m." I groaned, exhausted from all the fresh ocean air and lingering jet lag.

"I don't care. Get over here, these are good. You've got to see them."

*B*y the time I had collected myself and arrived at his cabin, Mac was already working on a sketch of the third hole. I entered in my sweat pants and received no greeting from Mac. He was in his "zone" I guess, because he just pointed to some drawings sitting on the corner of his desk.

"I've been on a roll," Mac said confidently. "Basically, I went over all of the many holes I've seen and built over the years, and tried to expand on the best of them."

Mac said that the brainstorming session brought back memories of his many projects, particularly those in the later years when he paid special attention to documenting his work. Mac had flipped through the worn, yellowed pages of his little black sketchbook, searching for the ideal green complex to begin the round at Pendleton Beach. He wanted something fair, but just tough enough to keep the good players on their toes.

"At some point I want you to turn these into presentable drawings, and do remember to keep some irregularity to the lines," Mac said. "I really hate those stiff-legged architectural renderings people do these days. Of course, they do fit with the drab, insipid look of the golf courses that are being built, so I guess I shouldn't be surprised!"

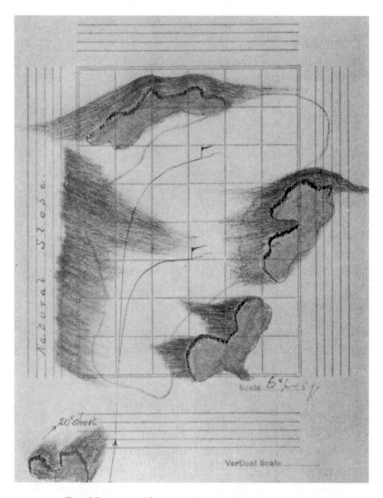

DR. MACKENZIE'S SKETCH OF THE FIRST GREEN,
PENDLETON BEACH.

The terrain for the first hole was pretty simple but Mac took advantage of the one primary feature. A twenty-foot-tall dune ran along the landing area on the left. It would make a perfect natural partition between the first and eighteenth fairways. Another gentle hillock sat about 250 yards from the tee, where Mac had already decided a bunker would be placed. He figured it would look good because it would be built into the mound, and it would serve a purpose in keeping the good players honest while being far out of reach for the average golfer. The wide fairway would also help many players overcome the traditional first tee jitters.

While I looked over the sketch, the Doctor returned to his sketchpad, drawing with the fervor of Mozart writing a symphony.

His sketch for the par-5 second hole fulfilled my expectations. He was going to build an adaptation of the famed Road Hole at St. Andrews, with the green perched right in front of the club entrance road as we had discussed.

Without critiquing the drawings, other than to say they looked great, I went back to my room and set about turning them into official sketches for the colonel and members to examine.

As I examined the first drawing more closely, I absorbed the Doctor's intentions for the opening hole. I was amazed at its strategic simplicity. Yet, few of my contemporaries were designing anything like it.

Instead of trying to duplicate Mac's artistic sketch, which really should have been left alone, I went back to bed and figured I would deal with the sketches after a good night's rest.

As good as Mac's sketch was, there was something bothering me. The idea that my first serious on-site golf course construction project depended on a tired old man who could die at any time worried me.

There was so much time between now and the completion of the project. What if Mac didn't make it? Would they have Bill Mario come back and finish it? That was too scary a thought to even consider.

15

$\mathcal{L}$ate October marked the end of four months at Pendleton Beach. Dan and Dave and their crew of six assistants had finished shaping most of the greens and bunkers. Only about five holes remained to be completed, and word had filtered out to the members that the course was making rapid progress. Though Doctor MacKenzie's exact whereabouts were apparently still unknown to the golf world, several publications ran investigative articles tracked his previous whereabouts as far as the Valley Club. There, the trail went cold. Though I knew it was only a matter of weeks before they found us.

From time to time some of the members would come by and try to strike up a conversation about the construction. Since I had somehow been transformed from the kid with the big mouth to resident diplomat, I was assigned to handle the members. Mac and the shapers had proven to be a little too impatient with the visitors, so my training as a modern-day publicist came in handy. But the project had also helped me grow as a designer. Even the Doctor conceded, usually after plenty of scotch, that several of the more interesting holes had benefited from my insight.

Dan and Dave built the course in numerical order from the first green to the second tee and on from there. Although the Doctor had done a rough sketch of the entire course, he produced his detailed drawings consecutively. Stakes had been placed at all of the green sites based on the initial routing. And though he seemed pleased with the progress of the course, the Doctor was struggling with the design of the finishing holes. Mac's indecisiveness and dwindling energy — a situation we were all aware of but did not discuss — became worse as the project wore on.

Dan and Dave's bunkers at Pendleton Beach defied imitation: a combination of MacKenzie's typical cape-and-bay, baseball-glove-shaped hazards mixed with an occasional deeper sod-faced pit. They resembled the puffy, wispy-edged clouds that passed by after the first rainstorm of the year, just as Mac had envisioned.

Once the bunkers were roughed out, I would seed the lips and surrounding areas by hand with fescue grass and monitor their grow-in. Within weeks the fringed look of the bunkers was stunning. Only Royal County Down had such awe-inspiring hazards.

At the end of four months, the first six holes had been seeded and were being mown. Irrigation was installed as soon as MacKenzie signed off on each green contour. Mac moaned a lot about overwatering — basically that was any distribution of water by the irrigation system that lasted over thirty seconds. Thankfully, the first autumn rains had revived the native fescue grasses, and the light topping of perennial rye and brown top bent was sprouting, creating emerald green fairways that would live off the ground moisture for most of the winter.

The membership hired a superintendent and a crew of four to maintain the holes and lend a hand from time to time with the construction. A temporary maintenance yard was erected near the second green until a permanent structure could be built.

Cottontail rabbits were turned loose on the new holes, and they soon took residence in the taller rough areas, spending their days nibbling on the new fairway turf. I couldn't tell if they really made a difference in the quality of the turf, but it sure made Mac happy to see the rabbits out there chewing away at the grass.

*I*t was an unusually windy and clear fall morning when I drove out early to watch Dan and Dave at work. While installation progressed on the irrigation system for holes seven through twelve, Dan and Dave were rough-grading the green complex for the par-3 thirteenth.

After a couple of hours I realized that Mac had not yet appeared. Though he had not been himself lately, this was strange — even for Mac. It was already nine o'clock, well past his normal sleep-in time.

Perhaps he was working on drawings for the final five holes. Lately, he had re-drawn each of the finishing holes several times in what I thought was an overzealous attempt to achieve perfection, but I hadn't mentioned it to him.

Jumping into my E-Z-GO cart, I drove to the cabins to check on the Doctor. After knocking on his door and not receiving any answer, I tested the door, discovered it was unlocked, and went inside. I found Mac passed out at his desk, still wearing his clothes from the day before. Judging from the odor pervading the cabin, I suspected he had worked the scotch a little too hard the night before. When I managed to shake him awake, I saw a pale and sickly old man with little of the old MacKenzie enthusiasm in his eyes.

"What's wrong, Doc?"

"Johnny, I'm not doing too well," he said, struggling to sit upright in his chair, his face as white as the bunkers at Augusta National.

"You just need some rest," I said, trying to reassure him and myself.

"No, no, Johnny. It's time for me to move on. Though I love what we are doing here, the work is killing me," Mac said, looking his age for the first time since we had met several months ago.

"Well, you can take a few days off," I said, trying to keep the sound of fear out of my voice. "Besides, we're making great progress."

"I'm not making progress," MacKenzie said with a morbid stare.

"What do you mean?"

"I'm tired. I have really struggled the last few weeks. And these final few holes have never been right. I'm further away than ever from getting them right."

"A little time off will do the trick, Doc. Trust me."

"No, John. If there is one thing I have learned in my 128 years, it's knowing when to move on." I could see the whole project collapsing in front of my eyes.

"You can't quit, Doc...not yet. This is the best course I've ever seen. Everyone who looks at it knows it is special, and we haven't even built the finishing holes."

"Johnny, it's your design to finish."

"What do you mean?" I cried, afraid to even think about the implications.

"Before I die, I want to take the Secretary at the Royal and Ancient up on his offer to visit St. Andrews one last time. Will you take me to the airport if I can get a flight to Edinburgh?"

"But you can't leave now..."

"You don't understand, Johnny, I have done all I can do. You're a fine architect, and you've been a fine student. I know if the members stay out of your way, the final holes will be in good hands with you and the boys. Do you think I would have enlisted you in the first place if I didn't think you were capable?"

$\mathcal{F}$ollowing more than an hour of pleas, arguing, threats and reassurances, I finally gave in and helped the Doctor pack his belongings. That afternoon I loaded up the Explorer and drove him to Los Angeles International to catch a nonstop flight to Edinburgh. From there, Mac could take a short car or train ride to his beloved St. Andrews.

Upon arriving at the airport, Mac handed me his old leather sketchbook. It contained most of his drawings, notes and sketches of dream holes from over the years.

"You keep this," MacKenzie said, pressing the sketchbook into my hands. "I hope you find some things in there that will help you finish the final holes. I think I am out of ideas."

"Wow! Thank you, Doc, I don't know what to say." I held the sketchbook reverently.

"Put it to good use."

"I will...thanks so much for everything you have taught me. I will never forget any of it." I hoped he knew how much I meant it.

"You'll do just fine, Johnny," MacKenzie said, patting me on the back. "Thank you for putting up with me and trying to teach me proper manners — you reminded me what it was like to be young again. I don't have what it takes to compete in your society. To be successful today, you have to be a salesman more than you have to be an expert, and I don't have the temperament or the training for that."

I just smiled. That was as close as the old man would ever come to admitting lacked diplomacy from time to time, but it was also an accurate commentary on the culture at the end of the twentieth century.

"Thank God for the Pendleton Beach men," MacKenzie continued. "They are good people. They know their place, and I'm sure that with your ideas, along with Dan and Dave's work, you'll do a fine job."

"What do you want me to tell people?" I asked, knowing full well that Colonel Murdoch and the others would know within a few days that Mac was gone.

"Tell them I have taken a trip to St. Andrews to get some fresh ideas from the Old Course."

Well, that was at least half true. "Do you want a progress report on the final holes?" I asked.

"You're bloody damn right I do! Send me letters in care of the Royal and Ancient Golf Club. The Secretary will make sure they get to me. Send me all of the final sketches and the routing, and in due time, photographs. If I last that long, I want to show the people at St. Andrews what a fine course we built."

With that, neither of us spoke another word. A skycap helped Mac with his suitcases, and a charming young lady from the airline greeted him with a special cart to take him to the terminal. As I shook his hand, I knew that we would never see each other again.

16

When Dan and Dave finished the green complex on the par-3 thirteenth they still did not know Mac had left. The thirteenth wound up being far different than we initially expected and would probably be considered the strangest hole by the Pendleton Beach golfers. The tee shot played slightly downhill, with one large bunker fronting the green. The putting surface itself was over 10,000 square feet, making it much larger than any other green on the course. There was one large hump in the back middle of the green, basically dividing it into two sections. It was built with lots of other little bumps and hollows throughout, in the spirit of the Old Course at St. Andrews.

Dan and Dave had carefully roughed out a tee for the fourteenth when they realized that there were no plans beyond the stakes marking its location and the direction of the hole. Neither Mac nor I had been around the construction area for several days. So, while Dave finished off the tee for fourteen, Dan came over to the cabins to investigate.

I, meanwhile, was doing my best Greta Garbo imitation by locking myself inside cabin number two at Pendleton Beach. Normally I'm pretty clean-cut, and I try to wear nice-looking golf clothes, but at the moment I was looking pretty sorry. I hadn't shaved or bathed in two days and had not set foot outside the cabin. Wadded up sketches littered the cabin floor, and an obnoxious daytime TV talk show blared unheeded in the background. It was not a pretty sight.

I heard Dan pull up his golf cart and knock on the door.

"What?" I asked, with no intention of opening the door.

"John, it's Dan. We're ready to build fourteen and fifteen. Are you and Mac ready to give us some instructions?"

I was going to have to open the door. "Just a minute," I called.

I tried hastily to clean up the room before letting Dan in. When I finally opened the door, the normally sober-faced shaper smiled when he saw that even the meticulous John Grant could let down his guard once in a while.

Instead of trying to make up some bogus story, I leveled with Dan. I told him about Mac's health and his departure for St. Andrews. Dan didn't seem surprised.

"So basically he has left it up to us to finish the project," I concluded.

"No problem, we just need to get rolling. Dave is getting antsy again," Dan chuckled.

"Um...the truth is..." I paused. "I...I have some sketches, but I'm not sure if they fit in with what we've built so far, or if they are what Mac would have wanted."

"Well, let me see 'em!" Dan said, actually sounding receptive to my ideas.

I handed him the sketch for the fourteenth.

"It's a 290-yard par-4, which I sort of designed in the spirit of some of my favorite short par-4's," I explained nervously. "If the pin is in the front, you can play any kind of tee shot you want. But if it is tucked in that little back right corner, you have to hit your tee shot down the left side. If the pin is in the back left, the best play is to hit a long tee shot down the right side."

Dan looked at the sketch for a long time. I couldn't tell from his expression whether he liked it or not. I waited anxiously for his reaction.

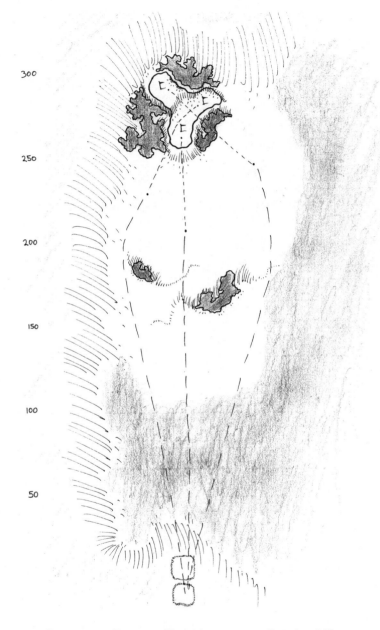

PENDLETON BEACH NO. 14   PAR 4   290 YARDS

"Would the Doctor want a two-tier green like this?" Dan finally asked.

"Funny you should bring that up," I answered, relieved that he had asked a serious question and one that I could handle. "I would have asked the same thing, but when I looked through his sketch book, I saw that he did it on the ninth at Cypress Point, so I figured it was all right. And I think he mentioned it as a possibility the first time we walked the site. The green site sort of lends itself to that kind of hole."

"Neat." Dan nodded his head and turned toward the door. "We'll get going on this one right now. Looks like a winner to me."

I couldn't believe what I was hearing. One of the great shapers in the world — one of the men who was so skeptical of me when we first met — actually liked it.

"Wait, I have another sketch for you to look at for the fifteenth," I said before he got away.

Dan skidded to a stop, turned around and took the sketch from my hand.

The fifteenth would probably play as the longest and toughest hole on the back nine. Mac had planned it that way, with the fourteenth and sixteenth holes being pretty short. Playing directly west toward the ocean, it was staked out at about 440 yards, but on most days the wind would corner from the north, making it play much longer for the average, slicing golfer. The green was patterned after Mac's Gibraltar hole at Moortown, a Redan-like complex where a smart player could utilize the wind and the slope of the ground on the approach shot.

However, because of the length of the second shot on fifteen, I did not include the right side bunkers found on the original Gibraltar. Instead, I placed additional bunkers on the left, rewarding the player who placed his drive on the right half of the fairway with an open view of the green.

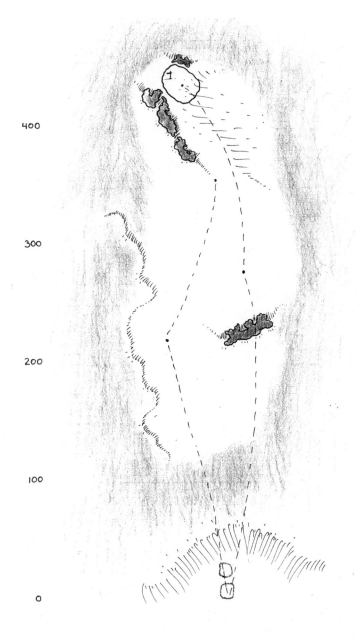

PENDLETON BEACH   NO. 15   PAR 4   440 YARDS

"My concern is that it will take a lot of dirt to build up the approach to the green," I said.

"Is that why you put this ridge on the left side of the fairway?" Dan asked, running his finger along some small slash marks on the page.

"Yeah, that was so you guys could cut some dirt from there. I also thought that it would make the fairway play a little tighter for the good player, especially when the wind is blowing."

"Looks good to me. This will keep us busy for a while," Dan said. And he left. Dan's casual acceptance of my design work was the ultimate compliment.

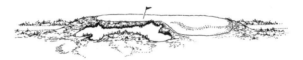

*O*ther than having to fend off Colonel Murdoch's questions with assurances that everything was fine and that Dr. MacKenzie was still involved, I was able to devote my attention to the finishing holes with a little more confidence. Dan and Dave were chugging away at the short fourteenth and the lengthy fifteenth, so the pressure was off for a few weeks at least.

I knew that if I put my best effort into the finishing three I would be able to make Mac proud and be able to say that I had a part in the finest course built in years. The burden, however, was mounting. The bottle of scotch that Mac had uncharacteristically left behind was looking more tempting by the hour. The more I stared at it, the more I believed that the Good Doctor just might have abandoned it on purpose, figuring I'd need it.

17

I spent most of my time in the cabin sketching out potential versions of the final three holes or watching Dan and Dave work their magic on fourteen and fifteen. I also spent countless hours sitting on the clifftops, surveying the ground for the sixteenth and seventeenth holes. Of all the holes to leave me with, Mac had to stick me with the ones everyone would study the most: the ocean holes.

To better attune myself to Mac's style, I reread *The Spirit of St. Andrews* and his first book, *Golf Architecture*. But the more I studied, the tougher it was to create an interesting set of finishing holes. I was starting to see why he was so frustrated.

I worried about Mac, but I knew the only thing I had any control over was the design of the finishing holes. I was in dire need of the Doctor's help, but I didn't know whether I should disturb him in Scotland — that is, if he was still alive.

While Dan and Dave were chipping away at the fifteenth, I flipped the "on" switch to my laptop and opened the word processing program. For the first time ever, I created "computer stationery" for the firm of "MacKenzie and Grant, Golf Course Architects."

I tried to remain humble, but the reality of the situation finally hit home when I typed "MacKenzie and Grant" at the top of the page. As I tapped away at the cramped keyboard, I kept reminding myself that I was in partnership with the most famous golf architect of all time. And now, on the biggest project of my life, my distinguished associate was halfway around the world — and possibly dead.

After hours of typing and retyping, I finished my letter to Mac. I printed it out and made the short drive north to the seaside town of San Clemente. There, I photocopied my sketches before air mailing the letter to Mac in care of the Royal and Ancient Golf Club, St. Andrews, Scotland.

MacKenzie and Grant
Golf Course Architects

November 12, 1998

Dr. Alister MacKenzie
Royal and Ancient Golf Club
St. Andrews, Fife KY16 9JD
Scotland

Dear Mac:

I hope this letter finds you well at St. Andrews. Enclosed you will find my sketches for numbers fourteen through eighteen. I tried to remain consistent with the thought behind some of your old drawings, especially on #14, where I based part of the green design on the ninth at Cypress Point.

You will find that #15 is a pretty basic hole, but I figured that as bizarre as sixteen and seventeen would be to the members, a conservative hole was needed at that point in the round. The par-3 over the ocean, #16, is going to be a large double-punchbowl green. I know what you are thinking—it's only 135 yards, but it is straight into the wind (some days you might need a wood to get there!) and actually there will only be a few pin placements. Since there is no room for a run-up approach, a more forgiving punchbowl green seemed to be the best solution. Your thoughts on a short forced carry hole for #16?

The seventeenth is based loosely on your eighteenth at the extinct Lido course, minus one of the landing areas off the tee. I have replaced the marsh areas that you had in your Lido hole design with bunkers for the Pendleton Beach version. This is similar to what we discussed while you were here, so I doubt you will object. I am most curious what your thoughts are on #18. It should make for an interesting finish, I think. Hopefully no one will get hurt by an incoming ball while they sit on the patio! Colonel Murdoch is having a four-foot stone wall constructed, and they will probably have some sort of awning over the patio area. It won't look too pretty, but it will keep the club lawyers happy.

I hope you made it to St. Andrews safely and that you will contact us soon. I am off to hit some shots from the proposed #17 tee site to determine if the different landing areas work!

Best wishes,

John

John Grant

~ One Pendleton Beach Road ~ San Clemente, California ~ 92672 ~ Phone/Fax: 714-555-0103 ~

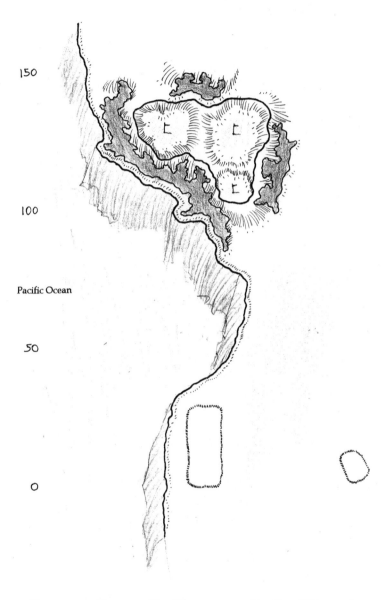

150

100

Pacific Ocean

50

0

PENDLETON BEACH   NO. 16   PAR 3   135 YARDS

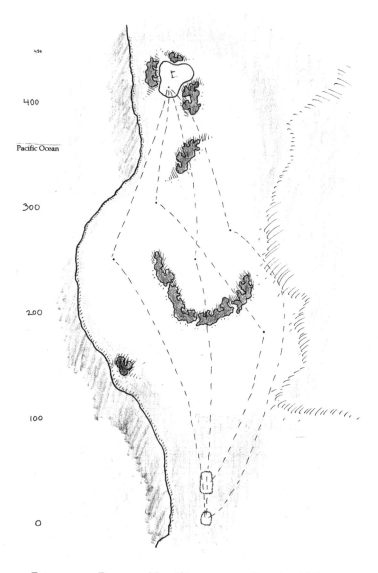

450

400

Pacific Ocean

300

200

100

0

PENDLETON BEACH   NO. 17   PAR 4   415 YARDS

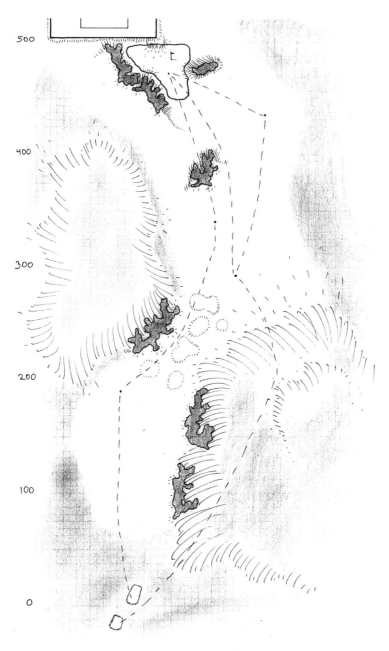

PENDLETON BEACH   NO. 18   PAR 5   510 YARDS

18

*I*t had been three weeks since I mailed my letter to the Doctor. In that time, Dan and Dave had finished building the eccentric fourteenth green and were nearly finished grading the fifteenth green. Normally fast workers, Dan and Dave understood how important MacKenzie's opinion was to me, so I think they deliberately took their time building the fifteenth, even stretching the work out through the four-day Thanksgiving break to give MacKenzie's reply time to reach me from Scotland. The break was the first vacation any of us had taken since the project began in July.

I had almost given up expecting a reply and was bracing myself to discuss the final three holes with Dan and Dave over dinner that night. The December days were getting shorter and the rainy season was approaching. We had to finish the final holes before the rains came in order to give the seed a chance to get established. While I was out by the cliffs taking a lunch break with the boys, Colonel Murdoch made an unannounced appearance on the construction site.

"Hello, fellas, how are things?" he said.

"Oh, fine," I said, jumping to my feet.

"Well, I don't want to bother you all, but I thought you might want to see this piece of mail as soon as it came in." I took a deep breath, preparing for the worst, until I turned the envelope over and recognized the loops and slants of Mac's familiar scrawl at the top, with a St. Andrews address written right below his name.

"Thank you, Colonel," I said, knowing that Murdoch now had a pretty good idea of what was going on.

Dan and Dave helpfully struck up a conversation with the colonel while they packed up their lunch boxes and prepared to go back to work a few feet away. After a couple of seconds of staring at the envelope, I pulled out my car keys and carefully slit it open.

DR. ALISTER MacKENZIE

December 8, 1998

Mr. John Grant
MacKenzie and Grant, Golf Course Architects
One Pendleton Beach Road
San Clemente, CA 92672

Dear John:

Thank you so much for your letter dated November 18, 1998. It appears that everything is going exceedingly well with the project as long as the rain stays away for just a few more weeks. I enjoyed your sketches, particularly those loose-edged lines. They are very reminiscent of my older work!

As for the holes, here are my thoughts. My only concern is that you seem almost obsessed with copying the principles of great holes which I have designed (with the exception of #16, which apparently is a C.B. Macdonald tribute!). Your primary goal should be to attempt to make every hole different and never to reproduce two exactly similar holes. Make sure you are getting your inspirations by seizing on any natural features and accentuating their best golfing points.

I point this out for future reference primarily. With that said, the short two-shotter, #14, is quite excellent. I am not a proponent of shelves in greens on a regular basis, at least not as often as you see them in your modern American courses. They discourage the run-up approach, but on a drive and pitch hole such as this one, it forces the player to plan from the tee where they want to place the tee shot. Excellent work, especially with the many options off the tee!

As for your fifteenth, the long two-shotter, I had reservations when first looking at your sketch. With that stiff afternoon breeze, I was afraid it might be a bit too difficult. I was dreading having to figure this one out, because there are simply no natural features on that portion of the property. But you did quite well with it. Just make sure the green is large enough.

On further review of the entire layout, #15 makes for a fine fit in the course of the round. We have three very reasonable par-5's that the good player will birdie more often than not, and I think a stern two-shotter is needed after the simplicity of numbers 11-14, which I view as all very birdieable if played properly.

I particularly liked your idea of the hollow ridge running the length of the left side of the fifteenth fairway. Remember that in constructing natural-looking undulations, one should study the manner in which those among the sand dunes are formed. I know that Dan and Dave understand this, but as I recall that portion of the property was so flat that any major undulation added to the fairway could look terribly out of place. Certainly Dan and Dave understand this principle, so I doubt it will be much of a problem.

Now to the sixteenth, or should I call it your "Ode to Charlie Macdonald." Surly old man he was; but who am I to talk! Anyhow, I support the idea of the green, I just hope that with these ridiculous modern green speeds, it doesn't become too severe. I built some rather bold contours at Pasatiempo on the eighth, ninth, sixteenth, and eighteenth holes, but with today's speeds they are much too severe to provide pleasurable golf.

Before I address the seventeenth, I must admit that I love the look of the front pin placement on #16, though on a windy day it could become a bit severe. Make sure to build plenty of green space up there, because the surrounding bunkers will encroach over the years. At some point, the green will become unputtable if the bunkers encroach too close to the green.

Your version of the seventeenth is a fine adaptation of the Lido #18 that won me the Country Life contest. This is the reason I was unable to finish the project, John. Here was a piece of ground screaming for an adaptation of the Lido hole, and I could not see it! Congratulations on a fine idea. We will be criticized for not using all of the oceanfront terrain, but there are two excellent holes along the coast, which sure beats three mediocre ones!

Do make sure to practice the tee shot on #17 under all wind conditions before grassing the hole. This is one that you want to execute well; it will be an embarrassment if the bunkers are out of reach, or worse, too easy to carry. Also, the right side ridge is used splendidly. Just don't shape it like a large chocolate drop — it would look horribly out of place so close to the coastline.

Now the finish! Interesting concept, though I must tell you, I don't know if I would want to eat lunch with my back to the fairway for fear of an incoming ball! I think it will make a fine finish, though it should be pretty simple for the good player when the wind is helping. Of course, these days the governing bodies all convert short par-5's into par-4's for championships, so I wouldn't worry about it being too easy. Tell your lawyer friends that the immense size of the green will deceive most of the players, and I suspect you will see very few balls hit into the clubhouse.

On #18 I particularly enjoy the landing area to the right of the green. It appears you will make the bunker over there quite deep. It also looks as if a player who hits a long, wayward second could actually be forced to chip over the patio! As long as you build up a nice berm to the rear of the green, the spectators should be safe, just as they are to the rear of the home hole at St. Andrews.

Incidentally, make sure that the player who tries for the big drive over the right hillock on #18 is penalized with some tall rough for a miss-hit. I know this contradicts our views on rough grass, but the hole will lack any intrigue for the low-handicappers if there is no danger and reward involved. I do see there is room behind the tee for more length should the weather conditions, or worse, equipment issues, force the hole to be lengthened.

In general, I can honestly state that you have designed stronger holes than I ever could have for the finishing stretch. I only wish I could play them. Please forward some photographs of the course as soon as possible.

My health has stabilized for the time being, and after this many years I can't complain. It is wonderful to be back here at St. Andrews. The people have welcomed me warmly, and the accommodations are excellent. One could talk for weeks about the Old Course, and I must say that to this day it gives the most lasting and increasing pleasure.

However, I have had to get a bit nasty about their practice prior to the Open Championship of making the players carry a little artificial mat with them to play their ball off of, so that the golfers don't put divots in the fairways. It is the most ridiculous idea I have ever seen, especially because it eliminates the challenges of shotmaking from bizarre lies.

Other than that, and this ridiculous looking high-rise hotel they built next to the Road Hole, the Old Course and the town of St. Andrews are just as I remember them. It is simply my favorite of all places in golf.

Please give my best to Colonel Murdoch, Dan and Dave, and the rest of the membership.

Yours Truly,

Alister MacKenzie

19

$\mathcal{T}$he winter had been kind to the course grow-in, with several gentle Pacific storms nurturing the grasses and sprouting the various grass seeds. A warm and relatively cloud-free spring prepared the greens for the first summer of limited play by the membership.

Dan and Dave had finished their work in early February. The final three holes evolved just as I had sketched them, and we seeded the finishing holes during the second week of February. Once the grass had sprouted on all eighteen holes, I toured the course and snapped over two hundred photographs to send to Mac.

While I took a vacation and supervised the grow-in of the course, I anxiously waited for a reply from the Doctor to my most recent letter and photos. Before I could relax and enjoy the experience of finishing my first design — well, four holes primarily — I needed Mac's approval. In the meantime, I read some of the back issues of the various golf magazines that had been piling up at the post office. I found out that Mac and I were the talk of the golf world!

Colonel Murdoch granted architect and writer Tom Doak and some *Golf Magazine* editors a June tour of the course, and they said it was good enough to enter their list of the Top 100 courses in the world. I welcomed friends in the architecture business that wanted to see the bunkers, though, curiously, no one from Bill Mario's office came by. Colonel Murdoch had to restrict access to the course just to prevent his phone from ringing off the hook for the next five years.

As opening day neared, the hype got so bad that several bigwig developers, who had been denied tours, rented helicopters to see the dynamic bunkers Dan and Dave had constructed. One golf publication even ran aerial pictures of the course with a monster headline that read, "Pebble Beach of the South?" I couldn't help laughing at it, but it was a nice compliment nonetheless. Still, there was the pressure of satisfying the most important people: the club members and their guests.

I went out with my clubs and played the course several times before Opening Day. I wasn't sure if it was my rustiness or the ocean wind, but I quickly learned that the course was a stern test. I knew that in the near future a few forward tees might be needed for the windy fall afternoons to keep some of the design strategy intact.

About a week before Opening Day and more than two months since I had sent Mac the final golf course photographs, a letter arrived from Scotland. It was a lengthy congratulatory note from Mac addressed to the membership. Clearly Mac had meant for the letter to be read on Opening Day.

"Doctor MacKenzie deeply regrets not being here," I told the July 1, 1999, gathering, my voice a little shaky. I was nervous partly because this was the first public speaking I'd done since high school, and to some extent because I wasn't telling the complete truth! "His declining health prevents him from traveling back here from St. Andrews," I finally concluded before passing the microphone over to Colonel Murdoch.

The one hundred Pendleton Beach members present for the opening were clearly disappointed. On the other hand, many were just eager to play the course. There was a mix of serious-looking golfers and part-time players dressed in everything from army fatigues to Ashworth shirts, and wearing shoes that ranged from top-of-the-line Foot-Joys to tattered tennis shoes.

"Though Doctor MacKenzie could not join us today, he sent the following letter," Colonel Murdoch proudly told his friends and fellow members from the Camp Pendleton base. "John will read it to you to inaugurate the golf course, and then it will be housed in the clubhouse for permanent display. I thank you for supporting the project and waiting patiently for this day to come, fifteen years after it all began. Special thanks to John Grant, the shapers Dan and Dave, and Alister MacKenzie for your devotion to our low-budget project."

I moved to the front of the podium again and pulled the envelope open to address the crowd, who sat in white folding chairs between the first tee and the practice range. I paused for a moment, making sure the group was settled in before reading the Doctor's three-page message:

DR. ALISTER MACKENZIE

June 12, 1999

Pendleton Beach Golf Links
One Pendleton Beach Road
San Clemente, CA 92672

Dear Friends and Golfers:

Congratulations on the completion of your most noble and wonderful project. The Pendleton Beach Golf Links will be a pleasurable test for many years to come. There are few problems more difficult to solve than the problem of what constitutes an ideal links or an ideal hole, but it is fairly safe to say that the ideal hole is one that affords the greatest pleasure to the greatest number. I am confident that each and every hole on your course fulfills that requirement.

Pendleton Beach will give the fullest advantage for accurate play, stimulate players to improve their game, and will never become monotonous. A good golf course is like good music or good art: it does not necessarily appeal the first time, but it grows on the player the more frequently he visits it. Please remember this in your early rounds if the course does not satisfy you. I would be concerned if you all walked off after your first round and considered it the most wonderful course you had ever played. It should, and will, grow on you.

It is an important thing in golf to make holes look much more difficult than they really are, and I think we have accomplished this at Pendleton Beach. People take more pleasure in playing a hole that looks almost impossible, yet is not so difficult as it appears. However, as I have suggested, it is no criterion of a good course that the course record be high.

On the subject of difficulty, I must also plead that you, the members, carefully consider any changes proposed for Pendleton Beach, and consult John Grant before proceeding. I rarely see an alteration to a golf course by a green committee that is a complete success. It would be wise for every club to have a permanent green committee. The history of most clubs is that a green committee is appointed and they then make mistakes. Just as they are beginning to learn from their mistakes, fresh members who make still greater ones replace them. You are very lucky to have a leader such as Colonel Murdoch

148

who is so knowledgeable in so many facets of the game. I hope you will trust all golf course related matters to him.

One of my great concerns with modern day golf is the alarming number of players who quietly give up the game. Yes, many are taking up the game, but equally as many are quitting. I attribute this to high costs in many instances. Yet the shabby architecture and the preposterous changes made by green committees surely have something to do with it. The golfer may never know this; he only knows that he is frustrated by the game and that he no longer derives pleasure from it. He doesn't know he should blame his dwindling incentive to improve his game on the poorly designed course he plays.

It is a remarkable thing about golf courses that nearly every man has an affection for the particular mud heap on which he plays. It is probably largely due to associations: his friends play there, he knows the course and can probably shoot a lower score there than elsewhere. He may also have pleasant recollections of the dollars he has won from his opponents. It may not even be a real course at all. There may be no interest or strategy about it; it simply gives him an opportunity for exercise and "socking" a golf ball. He is opposed to any alterations being made to it, but the time inevitably comes when he gets tired of golf without knowing why. Perhaps after spending a holiday on a good golf course, he clamors for the reconstruction of his home course, or he migrates elsewhere. I doubt that this will be the case with Pendleton Beach; it's the finest property I have ever seen for golf, with the exceptions of Cypress Point and the Old Course at St. Andrews.

Since I have already taken a good deal of your time I must also take a moment to urge you to reconsider your standards for modern-day fairway and approach maintenance. Let the rabbits take care of your fairways and mow the fairways only when the growing season is at its peak. I think you will be impressed with the turf if you trust the rabbits to work their magic.

If we never have a bad lie, we are not likely to appreciate a good one. Moreover, the ability to play from a bad lie differentiates between a good player and a poor one. Please put only the minimal amounts of water necessary on your course, and do not fret if there are brown or even, God forbid, yellow spots. Firm turf, the element of luck and bad lies are all part of the game. I might also point out that good and bad lies differentiate between the good sportsman and bad. If you want to find out if a man is a good trustworthy fellow or not, play golf with him and watch how he handles adversity!

The primary reason for the existence of golf and other games is that they promote the health, pleasure, and even the prosperity of the community. Please do not forget this. How frequently have I, with great difficulty, persuaded patients who were never off my doorstep to take up golf and how rarely have I seen them in my consulting rooms again.

Golf is a game, and talk, discussion, and even criticism (something forbidden with the architects today) are all in the best interests of golf. Anything that keeps the game alive and prevents us from being bored with it is an advantage. Anything that makes us think about it, talk about it, and dream about it is all to the good and prevents the game from dying.

In summary (I can hear your sighs of relief!), golf is a game and not a mathematical business. It is of vital importance to avoid anything that tends to make the game simplistic and stereotyped. On the contrary, every endeavor should be made to increase its strategy, variety, mystery, charm, character, and elusiveness, so that you shall never get bored with it. My hope for you, the members and guests of Pendleton Beach Golf Links, is that you are able to continue to pursue this game with increasing zest for the remainder of your lives.

Best wishes for fine golfing.

Yours Truly,

Alister MacKenzie

20

$\mathscr{T}$he crowd erupted in warm applause after I read Doctor MacKenzie's letter. The members seemed to genuinely enjoy what he had to say and I knew MacKenzie would be proud that his words had made an impact on the members of Pendleton Beach.

The friendly applause grew louder and louder, changing into the sound of a crowd cheering. My head felt strangely heavy. A bright light pressed against my eyes and I felt something slip off my lap. Slowly, I realized that my eyes were closed. I opened them to find that the annoying reading light next to my couch was shining into my tired eyes. My copy of *You Gotta Play Hurt* lay on the floor. My brain cells slowly came to life and I realized I was still wearing the clothes I'd worn to work. I wasn't at Pendleton Beach at all; I was at home in my own apartment.

Then I heard that weird voice coming from the television. I knew the voice but couldn't place it. What's his name?

"What stops us from taking action?" the deep voice said from the television set. Oh, no.

"Fear. Fear of failure, success, rejection, disappointment — unconscious fears we often don't even realize we have," he told the large studio audience with plenty of hand gestures to lure them in.

As he rambled on, full consciousness returned. I rubbed my face with my hands, tried to sit up straight and groaned as my cramped neck muscles protested. Yes, I was in my apartment, and everything was just as I remembered it. The television was on, and obviously I had been asleep on the couch all night. Holy Moses.

"To achieve true success, you must first break through fear," the man on the television said as dramatic film clips of him flying his helicopter around Hawaii replaced the audience on the screen. "You must also apply specific strategies for creating momentum in your life, so things that seemed difficult at first become easy over time. And third, develop the physical vitality and energy you need to follow through!"

I closed my eyes again, hoping to forget I had awakened, but the noise from the television set prevented a return to sleep. Pervading my stiff body was that early morning hangover feeling you get when you've been locked in an especially compelling dream. And that's what it all had been, a big dream. How unbelievably depressing.

Alister MacKenzie *was* dead. He had not lived to be 128, and he had not returned to golf course design. But wouldn't the world be a better place if he had, even if he were a gruff old Scot?

The realization that the Good Doctor had not in fact returned reminded me that I was still gainfully employed. And if I was still working for Bill Mario, that meant I had to be at work in a few hours. It's funny how slowly your mind works after a deep sleep.

I focused on the television screen again. Tony Robbins. That was the name of the man on the infomercial. I love this guy. He sits there for half an hour and provides hardly any tangible information. Yet, when he's finished, you're ready to go out and buy his tapes. Boy, is he good! And even though I don't agree with everything he says, his words started to sink in.

"Fear of failure, success...to achieve true success, you must first break through fear." I can't believe I'm listening to this guy. But he *does* have a point.

With surprise and disgust I realized I was afraid of Bill Mario. Afraid I couldn't survive without him. Afraid to be different and original. Afraid to deal with the truth that there is little pride to be gained in turning out second-hand rubbish. I'm afraid to tell people how an enduring golf course can be built with a little extra time and care for much less than the expected cost. But why was I afraid?

What would MacKenzie say? Would he tell me to quit and go to work for a company more in tune with my own thinking — or even try to succeed at golf course design on my own? Or would he want me to try to rehabilitate Bill Mario and teach him how to take advantage of his big budgets and his unique opportunities to build lasting courses?

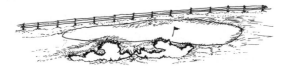

*J*t had been 5:30 a.m. when I awoke from the most significant dream of my life, and by 6:30 a.m I was faxing my resignation letter to Bill Mario. Doctor MacKenzie would not have had it any other way. He would have told me that I could make it in this business on my own if I'd just free myself from the constraints of safe employment and stick to my principles.

The resignation letter to Bill was pretty simple. I considered quoting that other philosopher named Robbins, Tom: "You've heard of people calling in sick. You may have called in sick a few times yourself. But have you ever thought about calling in well?

It'd go like this: you'd get the boss on the line and say, 'Listen, I've been sick ever since I started working here, but today I'm well and I won't be in anymore.'"

However, I like to think I'm above such sarcasm. And just in case my new career didn't flourish, I opted for a simple resignation letter and a big thank you for the opportunity to work with Bill over the last few years. Sure, it might have done Bill some good to hear what I really thought, but he was probably beyond rehabilitation.

21

$\mathcal{T}$he first few months of unemployment were wonderful. I lived off vacation pay that I had accumulated under Bill and took a trip to England and Scotland. I visited the Old Course at St. Andrews and all of Doctor MacKenzie's other original design work.

During my three-week stay in Scotland and England, I started going to antiquarian bookstores in search of first editions of old golf books. Even though I have all of the reprinted editions of the major architectural works, there is something about the thrill of finding just one first edition that keeps me going.

The trip to the Isles gave me a chance to ponder my options and review what had happened during the dream. I am not ordinarily the kind of person who analyzes or makes notes about a dream, but so much happened that night that I decided to enter an account of the dream into my computer. I realized that the fantasy of the Pendleton Beach project might serve as a useful model in the future if I ever did get a chance to work with a property of that caliber.

When I returned from the British Isles, I actually called the real Pendleton Beach to find out how their project was going. I even talked with *the* Colonel Murdoch. He wondered how I knew his name, and I reminded him of some of the articles over the years in which he had been quoted. He told me they currently had no architect under contract and that the project had little hope of getting off the ground. They weren't even going to interview anyone until they had some reason for hope, but I made sure to give him my name and address for when the day did eventually come.

Evidently, some organization of retired surfers with money to burn is claiming that they should be allowed to use the beach next to the golf course if the land is going to be developed for public use. Their claim is ridiculous and irrational since surfers have hundreds of miles of coastline for their activities. They are obviously using the golf course to further their own agenda as many of these groups do. I hope the colonel and his group eventually prevail, but with the current erroneous mentality that golf courses somehow have a negative impact on their surrounding environment, the prospects are dim.

Before my trip overseas I had started interviewing for jobs with several different architects, but I found that the opportunities were extremely limited. The architects I wanted to work for were not looking for anyone with as much experience as I had. They wanted a younger guy to answer the phones and deal with paperwork, not a design associate.

So I decided to open my own office and actually got a commission within a few months to design a par-3 course and driving range in Northern California. But I still had a lot of time on my hands, and my affection for used bookstores continued to grow.

During a visit to my parents' home in Palo Alto for Christmas, my mom recommended a few used bookstores to visit in my spare time. I had never noticed any of the places she mentioned while I was growing up, probably because I had no interest in books until I got to college.

The first store on my list was just a mile from my home in a charming two-story brick building near the Stanford campus. It was pretty dumpy inside, though, with books sitting in piles on the floor and dust and cobwebs in the corners. I found very few interesting golf books, but the general fiction section was pretty well stocked. Noticing that the sky was darkening with storm clouds, I started toward the door to leave, when an older gentleman, apparently the storeowner, asked if I was looking for anything specific.

"Yes," I said. "I'm looking for old books on golf, preferably golf course architecture related. Ever run across any such titles?"

The old man scratched his head, hoping to pry loose a thought stored deep in his brain. Then he smiled.

"There is one," he mused, trying to remember where he had last seen it. "Hold on one moment."

He pulled a set of keys from his pocket and walked over to a locked cabinet that I had noticed earlier but hadn't bothered to look into. He unlocked it and pulled out a small book. I immediately recognized it as a first edition of Alister MacKenzie's *Golf Architecture*, the first book he published, in 1920.

"How much is that one?" I asked coolly, trying not to betray my excitement. I noticed that the original dust jacket was still on the book and that it was in remarkably good condition. It was unusual to find the dust jacket on such an old book because buyers in the '20s used to discard the jackets from new books as soon as they got them. Dust jackets were viewed as a means to publicize other books by the publisher, not as a decorative part of the book design. That made antique books with their original dust jackets that much more valuable.

"Well, I suppose the book itself is worth about $300 because it's a first edition," the man said, sounding apologetic, "but I have to ask for twice that because it is signed."

The negotiations had begun.

"It's signed by the author?" I asked, knowing that if it was, the book was worth at least $3000.

"Yes," he confirmed, "and there is a letter by the author that is folded up in the back of the book. I've had this edition lying around here for several years now, so for you, how about an even $600?"

"I'll take it!" I said, forgetting to dicker and more curious about the letter than the book itself, though it would be nice to have a first edition MacKenzie. "Let me go down to the bank and get some..."

"That won't be necessary," the man interrupted, probably a bit surprised by my ready acceptance of his price. "I'll accept a personal check. You look like an honest young man."

"Well, thank you," I said, pulling out my checkbook. The bookstore owner started to wrap it up in tissue paper.

"That won't be necessary," I said appreciatively. "I'm going to read it right away."

J thanked him and hurried off to my car holding my prize purchase close to my chest. I got in and, for some reason, locked the door. I guess it made the moment seem more private. Carefully, I pulled the brittle letter out of the book. The yellowed stationery bore the name of "Dr. A. MacKenzie" at the top and listed his various associations around the country with Robert Hunter, Perry Maxwell and Alex Russell.

The letter was written to Jack Fleming, who designed several courses on his own and who had worked as MacKenzie's design associate for over twenty years. As the first raindrops spattered against my windshield, I sat back in the warmth and comfort of my Explorer and, in the fading light, read what had to be one of the last letters Doctor MacKenzie had ever written. It was dated January 2, 1934. He passed away on January 6.

DR. A. MACKENZIE

Golf Course Architect

AMERICAN PARTNERS

West of Rocky Mountains
Robert Hunter
Pebble Beach, California

East of Rocky Mountains
Perry D. Maxwell
Ardmore, Oklahoma

LONDON OFFICE

Moor Allerton Lodge
Leeds, England
Telephone 61990

Australian Partner
Alex Russell
Royal Golf Club, Melbourne

January 2, 1934

Mr. Jack Fleming
San Francisco Parks and Recreation
San Francisco, California

Dear Jack:

My health has been poor for some time now, so I thought I would write. I want to wish you the best in your endeavors. The world is very different these days for some odd reason and I dearly miss the old days when people read and studied more. But I know you will do just fine, Jack. You were always a fine student and worker.

It is strange that with all of the information our society has today, people seem less informed than ever. Then again, the course of mankind's progress does not run in a straight line, but is instead a struggle with bizarre, sometimes unexplainable detours. I am afraid that the golf architecture world is close to taking such a detour, with not the faintest idea how to get back on track. Most of the artistic endeavors I have seen lately indicate a society in a precarious state.

I hope the economic hardships we are all experiencing will improve and allow everyone to focus on their true passions. I sometimes wonder if America will ever recover from the devastation of this depression. I have not seen such widespread misery and suffering since the Great War and I fear it will forever change many Americans' passion for creativity.

I have read articles about some of the new men designing courses, and I am troubled to find that they are basing design decisions on little, if any, insightful information. You can always identify the second-handers. They quickly become defensive when you challenge them intellectually. Why? Because they never do any research nor develop any personal convictions, so they are left with only their muffled view of life.

The new generation, and perhaps this is a product of these tough times, seems to want to discourage enlightened thought, constructive criticism or intelligent discussion, which I might point out are all methods to improve society. Isn't an enhanced society what we all desire?

Golf architecture is still a new art form, closely allied to that of the artist or sculptor or certainly the master landscape architects, but it also necessitates a scientific knowledge of many other subjects. I just hope that the scientific side never dominates the artistic and strategic sides.

I wish you the best of luck, Jack. I am happy to hear that your position with the Parks Department is working out. It will provide you with some security until the economy improves, and I hope that you will then have the opportunity to create your own architecture practice.

Jack, be strong in your faith and convictions, and don't worry about what misinformed others say about your work. Remain curious and never lose your desire to learn and to understand. Lead by example and do not let the criticisms of second-handers discourage you from doing what is best for the greatest number of golfers. You have come a long way from the day we first met, and I am satisfied that you will have a productive career.

As for me, I have certainly lived a unique and complete life. I regret how I treated certain people in my earlier years, and only hope that the Lord doesn't discipline me too harshly! I am proud of the many associations I have had and of the advances men like you have made. You were just a young lad when we hired you for the project at Manchester, and I greatly appreciate your loyalty over the years. I have entrusted many of my personal affairs to Hilda, but I hope you will continue to keep a watchful eye on our design work. I hope that the courses we built will survive as we have left them, but I have seen too many green committees disregard rational thought in an effort to appease their egos.

My fondest memories will be of two places: St. Andrews, which to this day defies imagination or imitation, and Pasatiempo, where I enjoyed many wonderful moments with Hilda and where I have had a unique association with Marion Hollins. Pasatiempo was built to challenge and entertain the average player. It's the average players who make the game what it is.

They pay the bills, and they are the ones who bravely keep coming back in that quest for just one day of perfection. Don't ever forget them in your design work.

Best wishes for a full and prosperous life!

Yours truly,

Alistair MacKenzIe

P.S. — Pleasurable exercise and a steady diet of Scotch are the secrets to a long life — don't believe anyone who tells you otherwise.

Acknowledgments

*A*s with any completed golf course design, this book could not have been finished without the support of many people. A world of thanks to all of those who read the manuscript and offered sage advice: Yancey and Claire Beamer, Ben Crenshaw, Bill Coore, Bradley Klein, Steve McHugh, Tom Naccarato, my parents Lynn and Diane, my grandparents Ray and Louise, Eric Shortz, Karen Smith and Daniel Wexler. Most of all, I'd like to thank Saundra Sheffer, whose editing prowess and vision helped immeasurably.

Though it must have been somewhat awkward for him to read, I must sincerely thank Alister MacKenzie's step-grandson Raymund Haddock for patiently reading the manuscript, pointing out any historical discrepancies and supporting the concept of the book.

Special thanks to all of those who offered practical or historical information: Dave Axland, George Bahto, Bob Beck, Norm Bernard, Terry Buchen, Todd Connelly, Tom Doak, John Fleming, Ross Forbes, Alex Galvan, Bruce Hepner, Dan King, Jim Langley, Iain Macfarlane-Lowe, John Marvel, Sid Matthew, Patty Moran, Fred Muller, Dan Proctor, John Rydell, Jim Urbina, Ron Whitten and so many others who I've met along the way in search of great golf courses.

I'd also like to thank a talented golf architect and artist, Mike DeVries, for his drawings that so beautifully separate the text throughout the book.

Finally, I must recognize a man I have never met but surely wish I could: Doctor Alister MacKenzie. He left a thorough collection of writings to base this book on, and I hope he would agree that his thoughts have been well-represented. His epic books, *The Spirit of St. Andrews* and *Golf Architecture,* were used extensively throughout to create most of Doctor MacKenzie's dialog and philosophy, though most of the excerpts were modified to create more coherent dialog or to address contemporary issues.

~ Pendleton Beach Golf Links ~
San Clemente, California
Designed by Dr. Alister MacKenzie and John Grant

Hole	Name	Par	Back Tees	Front Tees
1	Pacific Bound	4	360	350
2	Road Hole	5	520	490
3	Dan and Dave	3	210	195
4	Strategy	4	410	390
5	Boomerang	4	300	285
6	Redan	3	165	150
7	Beardies	5	580	550
8	Hillocks	4	445	425
9	Valley of Sin	4	310	300
Out		36	3300	3135
10	Patty Cole	4	435	415
11	Four Corners	5	535	505
12	Blind	4	385	360
13	Tom Morris	3	185	170
14	A-Frame	4	290	280
15	Westward Ho!	4	440	420
16	Punchbowl	3	135	120
17	Lido	4	415	390
18	Patio	5	510	495
In		36	3330	3155
Total		72	6630	6290

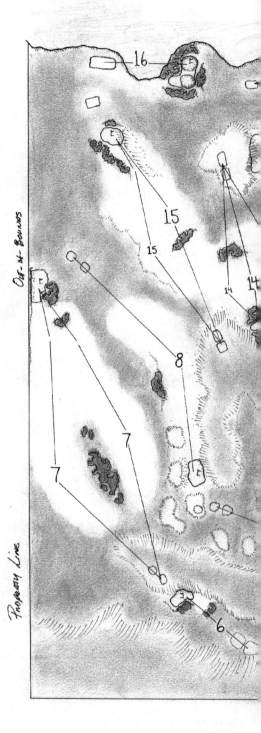